I0152839

THE SAINT AUGUSTINE LECTURE SERIES

Augustinian Institute
Villanova University

Saint Augustine and
the Augustinian Tradition

EDITOR

Robert P. Russell, O.S.A.

ASSOCIATE EDITORS

Russell J. DeSimone, O.S.A.

Benedict A. Paparella, Ph.D.

THE SAINT AUGUSTINE LECTURE 1973

AUGUSTINE'S STRATEGY

AS AN

APOLOGIST

EUGENE TESELLE

WIPF & STOCK · Eugene, Oregon

Wipf and Stock Publishers
199 W 8th Ave, Suite 3
Eugene, OR 97401

Augustine's Strategy as an Apologist
The Saint Augustine Lecture 1973
By TeSelle, Eugene
Copyright©1974 by TeSelle, Eugene
ISBN 13: 978-60899-871-5
Publication date 7/22/2010
Previously published by Villanova University Press, 1974

CONTENTS

AUGUSTINE'S STRATEGY

AS AN

APOLOGIST

AUGUSTINE'S STRATEGY
AS AN APOLOGIST

In 1777, in the midst of a new dispute over the historical criticism of the gospels, Lessing wrote a famous little paper in which he made the point that historical assertions about miracles and fulfilled prophecies may not be as valuable as apologists for Christianity had often supposed. The difficulty, he said, is that historical reports cannot be a proof of the metaphysical and moral claims made by Christianity; that would be to jump from one set of meanings to another.

But Lessing seems to hold out another possibility. The motto of this little writing is a passage from the beginning of Origen's reply to Celsus, where Origen asserts that

> the gospel has a proof which is peculiar to itself, and which is more divine than a Greek proof based on dialectical argument. This more divine demonstration the apostle calls a "demonstration of the Spirit and of power."

By Spirit Origen means not charismatic gifts but prophecies fulfilled in Christ; by power he means miracles. What interests Lessing is that Origen finishes by saying,

> traces of them [miracles] still remain among those who live according to the will of the Logos.[1]

The demonstration of the Spirit and of power, Lessing suggests, occurs whenever one actually *experiences* a miracle or the fulfillment of a prophecy;

1

even this, however, does not help him greatly, since he lives in the eighteenth century, and no longer experiences such things. But he still has one thing left—the teachings themselves, the recognition that has been given to them, their fruits in human life.[2]

Without taking Lessing as an authority or attempting to say exactly what he meant, I wish to pick up the theme which he brought out. For it is an important strand not only in modern justifications of the Christian faith, which characteristically try to avoid pure argumentation and come as close as possible to direct experience and insight,[3] but also in patristic apologetics. Although the writers of that age could engage in all the familiar kinds of argumentation—the nature of human knowledge, the existence of God, the destiny of man, the need of revelation and salvation—they could never stray far from their immediate situation of encounter with government, pagan religion, and the philosophers, where the Christian movement had to make good its claims through comparison or combat with its surroundings.

Take Origen, since Lessing seems to have learned something from him. He exploits the fact that the apostles were simple men, deficient in learning, for this shows that they relied not on the wisdom of men but on the power of God. He often takes note of the way they lived and risked death and endured suffering, as proof of their conviction of the truth of what they were proclaiming; and he contrasts them with the philosophers, who teach many of the same truths about God and the soul

2

but are able neither to live as though the things they say are true, nor to bring others to live in this way.[4]

Origen is not glorifying mere fanaticism or blind faith. He is able to bring some clear criteria to bear—the philosophical one that thousands have abandoned the merely customary religion of their own cultures to follow, despite all the dangers, a truly rational and spiritual faith; the moral one that there has been a dramatic conversion or rectification of life; and the religious one that all of these things are worthy of God, showing his love toward the human race by communicating with them in a way they can understand and helping them for their own benefit.[5]

It is the same with Augustine. Although he wrote on the whole range of apologetic themes,[6] his apologetics usually comes to a focus in an encounter of life with life, evaluated in the light of moral and religious criteria which can be made clear to all. The proof of Christianity is in the moving of the Spirit. But the gifts of the Spirit are authenticated only if they conform to the moral norms which issue from the eternal Word; and the test, quite simply, is the love of God and of one's neighbor in God.[7]

But on the way to and from that focal point (and it is a point upon which he touches repeatedly) Augustine has much else to say, and it must be attended to if we are to understand even this criterion of love properly. I propose to follow him through three periods, noting how his concerns—

and his apologetic methods—shift in important ways. If I may be somewhat schematic, early in his career his manner is what was called in that era "protreptic" or hortatory, a friendly kind of discourse urging one's readers to follow out their own best insights, almost what we call today "dialogue"; and he addresses himself especially to those who had some philosophical training or sympathies. In mid-career his style shifts to what was called "eristic" or controversial; his attack was on the religious front, against the pagans and their philosophical admirers. And at the last he finds, in *The City of God*, that he must write an *apologia* in the strictest sense, a defense and justification of the Christian community; and it had to be addressed, as in the days of the first apologists, to those who considered themselves the champions of the Roman system of government. As Augustine moves through these stages the changes come not through subtracting anything essential but rather through adding new complications, so that he ends with a chastened apologetic strategy which, I shall suggest, still deserves our attention today.

I. Exhortation to the Philosophers

The early Church did not feel compelled to devote a major effort, in the fashion of most Christian apologetics since Thomas Aquinas, to arguments about the range of human knowledge, the existence of God, and the destiny of the soul. To be sure, the philosophical schools had their disagreements, and Christian writers shared in the debate; Augustine even made some notable contributions by way of philosophical argumentation on these questions.[8] But the philosophers who counted in their eyes—the Stoics in at least some respects, the Platonists in even more—were already professing doctrines full of religious import concerning God and human destiny. Although Christian writers had much to say in criticism and correction of these philosophers (and the Christian transformation of ancient philosophy is one of the important topics in patristic studies), just as often we get the impression that they make an effort to interpret them for the better, bringing them as close to Christian doctrine as they can, and if that is not possible they let their teachings stand as a rough approximation to the truth, sufficient evidence that the philosophers have apprehended the same realities that the Christians speak of and, conversely, that Christian belief has an intellectual respectability that should impress both critical outsiders and wavering believers. The enthusiasm of Justin Martyr and Clement of Alexandria over Plato is notorious; and Augustine scarcely falls short of them in his admiration for Plotinus, who he always believed had an essentially correct apprehension of the Trinity, and for Porphyry, whom he calls the noblest of the philosophers.[9]

The deepest stratum in Augustine's utterances about the philosophers, then, is one of agreement with their quest for true wisdom and of admiration for what they were able to achieve. But their achievement was largely one of knowledge, not of life. His favorite image is that the philosophers are able to see the goal—that is, they are aware of God, they know that their fulfillment can consist only in union with God, they even know that the journey to be taken is not one for ships or chariots, as though God were distant, but for the affections, becoming pure in heart and apprehending the God who has always been present—but they are not traveling the way that actually leads there.[10] The chief task of apologetics in the patristic situation (and it may be similar in our day, with its resurgence of religious and philosophical quests) was not to build up more elaborate speculations but to ask whether people had followed the light they already had. Augustine reproached the philosophers for not having the courage of their own convictions: they understood the one God, but they continued none the less to worship according to popular superstition. The problem comes to a focus, then, in their lack of wholehearted dedication and heroic courage, while the Christians, whom they scorned as ignorant, were actually leading the life glimpsed in its essential outlines by the philosophers.

This line of argumentation is all the more important because it was the major factor in Augustine's own conversion to Christianity, so far as we can puzzle out his thoughts at the time. He had been drawn to philosophy at the age of nineteen, and it affected his many changes of opinion from that time on. He remained proudly outside the Catholic Church, hoping to find a religion of reason rather than authority, and when he went to Milan in 384 as a professor of rhetoric it was with the recommendation of Symmachus, the leader of the pagan opposition to the Christianization of the Empire, who was probably glad to find a cultured, philosophical man unfriendly to the Church.[11] Two years later he decided to become a Catholic Christian.

It will strike us as strange that Augustine was never impressed by the political courage of Ambrose, though he went to Milan in the year of the climactic struggle between Symmachus and Ambrose over the removal of the altar of the goddess Victory from the Senate building, and his conversion came in the year of the controversy over giving a basilica in Milan to the Arians, when Ambrose and his followers were even besieged in one of the churches for a time by the Emperor's own troops. But Augustine never was inclined toward political opposition, and at the time of his conversion he was preoccupied with God and the soul. The heroism that counted was that of which he heard in stories about Marius Victorinus, the rhetorician who found his philosophic quest fulfilled when he stopped defending pagan religion and humbled himself in baptism, or Antony, the monk who showed the way to a new form of dedication which could vie with that of the martyrs, or the two young men who gave themselves to the monastic life after happening upon the life of Antony in distant Treves, or the community of monks right outside the walls of Milan. It was this life of contemplation and striving after perfection to which Au-

7

gustine devoted himself after his conversion, and it is evident from the record that he had been persuaded by the heroic lives of the Christians that their religion, far from being contrary to the philosophic ideal, was indeed its actualization.[12]

Augustine was impressed with the massive exodus of philosophic spirits like himself from a spiritual servitude in Egypt, bringing with them the gold of a Gentile philosophy that had always belonged to God; therefore he felt that the best of this philosophy leads properly into Christianity—not easily, by a natural development, since it must be through a sometimes agonizing conversion, and yet appropriately.[13] He even has a historical theory about the Platonists. They had the right views about being, truth, and goodness; but knowing that the majority of people would believe the Stoics and Epicureans, and having only human authority, they chose to conceal their teachings under the facade of Academic doubt, contenting themselves with attacking the views of their opponents. It was only after Christ began to be preached that Plotinus openly taught, once again, the doctrines of the Platonists. And increasingly the Platonist philosophers have submitted to Christ, "at whose command," Augustine concludes, "the truth which they feared to publish was immediately believed."[14] He even imagines Plato coming to life again. Certainly he would become a Christian, as many of the Platonists have done. And why? Because he would recognize that his own dialogues were more pleasant to read than they were potent to persuade.[15]

The problem, then, is their lack of authority or persuasiveness. And it is not to be solved with mere rhetorical ability. It lies at a deeper level than that. The indictment, as we have seen, is that they lacked the courage to follow out their own principles to the point of going counter to popular opinion, making an issue of them, and urging others to follow.

But Augustine is not a mere scold, rebuking the philosophers for cowardice as though a little more nerve could have put them across the line. His first impulse is to speak of them more in pity than in anger, for they only did what is to be expected of those who operate on the basis of human conjecture. Their knowledge of God and of the soul's proper destiny was, after all, merely a glimpse, and their doctrines, while basically correct, were still a vague approximation, as all human formulations must be, leaving much room for uncertainty and controversy.[16] Thus the lack of heroic achievement results from a lack of certitude, and this, in turn, results from an absence of sure knowledge. The resolution must lie in gaining some other source of certitude; and this substitute for direct knowledge is authority. If we cannot experience something directly, we can still be told about it by someone whose testimony can be trusted.[17]

Authority, then, is what arouses conviction, which in turn strengthens the will so that a life is led in keeping with one's professions. Because this entire sequence holds together, the authority of which he speaks is not arbitrary, and it need not be accepted blindly, without an understanding of its value and its consequences. In the lives of the Christians there is a confirmation or reinforcement of the message they proclaim. Authority itself often seems to be understood as correlative, involving acknowledgment as part of its meaning. And once it takes effect in responsive lives, these lives even share something of that same authority.[18]

One of the influential but much debated features of Augustine's thought is his insistence upon the authority of the Church. He has come to believe in Christ, he says, only through its mediation, indeed, by its "authority";[19] and he even utters the famous statement, "I would not believe in the gospel unless the authority of the Catholic Church moved me."[20] We should be careful with such texts. They are scarcely a theory of the magisterium, but belong to apologetics, specifically to his controversy with the Manichaeans, and are calculated to score a double-edged debating thrust: in an autobiographical vein he explains why he feels bound to continue within the Catholic communion through which he first learned to believe in Christ, and which continues to hold his loyalties in many ways; and at the same time he denies his opponents any right to use the Scriptures for their own purposes, since these were first possessed by the Church.[21]

Despite this qualification, it still remains true that Augustine cites, in proof of Christian claims, a whole series of facts—"the predictions of the prophets, the incarnation and teaching of Christ,

the journeying of the apostles, the reproaches, cros-
ses, blood, and deaths of the martyrs, the laudable
lives of the saints";[22] the remarkable expansion of
Christianity throughout the world, converting the
multitudes, uniting many peoples;[23] the continuity
of bishops, the see of Peter, the name "Catholic"
which is acknowledged even by opponents.[24] All
of these have apologetic force.

These phenomena do not as such bear authority
within themselves. Even the authority of the
Church is not identical with its continuity or its
geographic extent. They are rather a direct and
immediate confirmation of the authority of the
message that is proclaimed, the *divine revelation*
that is now being read to the peoples and is being
heeded by them.[25] The difficulty of Plato and the
other philosophers was, as we saw, that they were
not able to *persuade*; and the persuasiveness of the
Christian *message* is what is central to authority
as Augustine understands it, reinforced by these
symptoms of its effectiveness. It is the message,
the teaching, the will and the promises of God that,
beginning as divine authority, can also become
authoritative in the mouth of the Church and of
all Christian people—but only, it would appear,
when they can be seen to have taken effect in
responsive lives.

This is Augustine's version of the "demonstration of the Spirit and of power." He is never
content to point merely to impressive phenomena
within the human realm, as though they will be
self-authenticating. They must be in accord with

11

the best wisdom that men can arrive at, whether through reason or revelation, and Augustine is willing, as Origen was, to let them be judged by those standards. But those standards by themselves would be useless if they did not bear fruit in human lives. The Spirit is not to be found apart from the Word, nor the Word without the Spirit; but the proclamation of the Word is authoritative precisely because it carries along with it the power to persuade and convince and call forth the action of the heart.

II. Attack on Pagan Religion

During the writing of the *Confessions* (about 397 to 400) Augustine's tone changes. Without dropping his praise for the Platonists, he adds some new and harsher criticisms of them, and especially of Porphyry, a contemporary of Plotinus who admired him but took a much greater interest than Plotinus in the myths and rituals of Greece, Egypt, and Chaldaea, and also engaged in a vigorous and well-informed criticism of Christianity.

For some reason Augustine now begins to debate in earnest with Porphyry and his contemporary followers. Perhaps it has something to do with the climactic religious struggles of the 390's, when the pagan forces seized control of the government in Rome for a brief period and then were decisively crushed by Theodosius and his sons. Augustine comments a number of times that paganism is on the wane; the chief holdouts seem to be a few educated people with philosophical pretensions and a loyalty to old traditions, and he taunts them with not having the courage to come out openly, but muttering in private and spreading doubt where they could. This is the period of Augustine the triumphalist, who, in the spirit of the times, goes on the attack against pagan religion.[26]

With greater frequency than before, Augustine charges the philosophers with pride, attempting to reach true happiness by their own powers. Like Paul denouncing works-righteousness, he is especially harsh on those who have heard but rejected the way of salvation that has been offered in the humble Christ.[27] What may have been inevitable before the proclamation of Christ is totally inexcusable after that message began to reach everyone's ears. And they have not merely rejected the true mediator; they have been deceived by false mediators, the pagan gods who are really daemons; under the guise of leading their worshipers toward the supreme God they actually keep them under their own power and entangle them more deeply in guilt.[28]

But Augustine is not merely criticizing a few philosophers. His assault is along a much broader front, for he, like earlier Christian apologists, had to confront the entire religious policy of classical culture. It was a matter of a tolerant pluralism against a radical monotheism; pagan inclusiveness against Hebraic exclusiveness. The philosophers were not the only defenders of that religious policy, merely the most culpable, since they should have known that the supreme God does not wish his worship to be shared with others. But they chose to compromise. At best they refrained from criticizing popular religion; at worst they took delight in studying it in all its details, interpreting it as favorably as possible, and urging others to engage in magic, the sacrifices, and the mystery cults.[29]

The typical argument of the pagans was that there are many ways that lead toward God. The classic statement, once again, was from Porphyry, who said that no "universal way of salvation" had come to his attention, either through historical knowledge or through philosophy. But this notion that there are many ways to God was also thrown up against Augustine by contemporary pagan correspondents as well.[30]

Augustine, with a sure instinct, finds the fissure in their position and exploits it to the full. Let us assume this tolerant pluralism, he says in effect, and grant that every nation ought to worship its gods according to its own traditions, and that respect should be given to them all. That same principle must include, therefore, the Hebrews and the God of the Hebrews. Indeed, a number of philosophers have singled out this God of the Hebrews for special honor, and even their oracles praise him as a great God, showing that the daemons tremble before him.[31] Why, then, do they not worship this God? If they fail to worship him, they are not consistently following their policy of worshiping all gods. But they know, of course, that if they worship this God as they should they cannot worship the other gods, and so they are caught on a dilemma. The Hebrews, then, being one nation among others, have been able to get within the enemy camp and, once there, be a constant irritant and reproach to the rest of them.[32]

This is the scandal of particularity, and Augustine is ready, as we shall see, to assert it with some belligerence. Lest we think of him as merely intolerant, however, we should note that during these same years he was trying to come to terms with the diversity that was obvious even *within* the body of those who worshiped the God of the Hebrews—a diversity in space, since the Catholic Church included many peoples and followed many different traditions,[33] but even more a diversity across time, reaching behind the Church to Israel, and to the believing Gentiles mentioned in the Scriptures, and behind Israel to the patriarchs and other righteous persons from the beginning of the human race. It was during these years that Augustine began developing the notion that two spiritual cities had existed from the first, so that the *ecclesia* began with Abel and grew throughout human history, the body preceding Christ the head, or, to change the metaphor, the patriarchs and prophets being like a hand thrust forth before the head and the whole body are born.[34]

Therefore when a deacon in Carthage wrote to tell him about some scoffers (obviously influenced by Porphyry) who were asking, "If Christ is the only way of return to God, what about those who lived in earlier times, when a variety of gods was worshiped, or what about those who lived even

15

before the promulgation of the law of Moses, which was relatively late and was limited to a small area?" Augustine was able to take the objection in stride. He affirmed once again that "from the beginning of the human race" the Word has never ceased to speak and believers have never been lacking. The pagans' favorite argument, that there must be a variety of rituals adapted to different times and places, can be used, he says, by the Christians as well. From the beginning of the human race the same God has been worshiped, with the same "religion" or the same "faith," and the only difference is in the rituals, which vary according to what is suited to the circumstances. Thus the Christian objection to paganism is not that it has a diversity of rituals—this is an objection, he acknowledges, which can be made against *every* religion—but that it has not worshiped the true God. Likewise the Scriptures do not object to temples and sacrifices as such, for Israel itself worshiped in this way, but only to their use in the worship of idols and daemons.[35]

The grace of God spreads a wide umbrella over human kind. But its tolerance for diverse *forms* does not extend to tolerance in the *worship itself*. The criterion is a stern one: God does not share worship and sacrifice with any others, and even the angels (whom Augustine is willing to call "gods" in keeping with Biblical and classical usage) will refuse to receive worship, for they consider men and women their fellow citizens, and in the egalitarianism of God's city even believers can be called "gods." Therefore the daemons or any alleged gods who claim worship for themselves cannot be mediators to the supreme God but are deceivers; the only true mediation between God and man is always after the pattern of Christ, a mediation that does not stand in an intermediate position but rather joins the extremes in an immediate union and interpenetration.[36]

Augustine could not help rejoicing in the legislation of Theodosius and his sons forbidding pagan sacrifices and closing the temples. But when an anguished cry went up from the pagans after these laws began to be enforced in Africa in 399 (and the cry did go up, as we can see from the volume of his correspondence and controversial writing), he had to justify these actions of Christian rulers. In addition the Donatists, who were already feeling government pressures, were asking whether it is proper for Christians to accept help from Caesar. Augustine's strategy, quite in keeping with his general posture of attack, is what we might call *juristic*, for he characteristically seeks arguments in divine law giving to rulers in Christian times the *right* to exercise such measures.

The pagans were able to point out that Christ himself never expressly prohibited the worship of other gods or commanded that images be broken (perhaps the pagans had been listening all too well to Christian depictions of Jesus after the model of a Greek philosopher rather than a Palestinian Jew). Augustine's defense is that "the God of the Hebrews" commanded these things—once again the

17

presence of the Jews, with the Scriptures in their hands, is useful to his argument—and, furthermore, that this same God not only commanded them but promised through his prophets that the commands would be fulfilled in the future, and now, through Christ, he has become the God of all the earth and is in the process of fulfilling those prophecies.[37]

The rapid worldwide expansion of Christianity was one of the classic arguments of Christian apologists, and Augustine had already made use of it earlier, as a kind of "moral miracle" authenticating Christian claims.[38] But now it becomes an argument from prophecy, the kind of argument from prophecy that might even satisfy Lessing, or at least satisfies Lessing's criterion that one must see prophecies being fulfilled within one's own experience.[39] The purpose is not so much to validate Christianity as such, as to justify current events, reinforce the feeling of triumph, show that those who hold back are utterly without excuse after what they have seen, and overwhelm them by pointing to the multitude of Christians.[40] The dispute was not, after all, over the academic question whether the expansion of the Church is a fulfillment of prophecy but over the political one whether the Church should countenance the intervention of the state and the use of force against its enemies. Both the pagans and the Donatists exploited this point to the full, and Augustine showed by his defensiveness that he felt its force. His reponse was to turn the objection around and make it one more weapon in his justification from prophecy. The prophets foretell the destruction of the idols, and since this is something that can be done lawfully only by rulers, we may have confidence that the Christian emperors are acting in accordance with God's will; indeed, it is explicitly foretold that the kings of the Gentiles will serve the God of Zion.[41]

The use made of this Scriptural ammunition can appear crass and brutal. Perhaps it is that at times. But the horror is the horror of a moral warfare which must simply be accepted as a fact.

Always the evil have persecuted the good, and the good have persecuted the evil.[42]

Retribution now has its turn.

Babylon, when she could persecute the Christians, killed their flesh, though she could not harm God; now they return to her double, for pagans are destroyed and idols are smashed. How, you will say, are pagans killed? How except that they become Christians? I look for a pagan, and I do not find one. He is a Christian. Therefore the pagan is dead.[43]

The change has come about in open battle, with unequal forces, naked power against righteousness. What the three youths demonstrated to Nebuchadnezzar, and the Christians to the emperors, is that "the faithful liberty of the saints cannot be overcome either by royal power or by savage punishment," and because of this the rulers were converted.[44] The new policies, Augustine claims, are animated by a different spirit. The rulers, subdued "not by resisting but by dying Christians," now count it their highest honor to kneel at the tomb

19

of the fisherman; for the Christ who rules the earth is still not a Christ with worldly honors, wealth, or happiness, but Christ crucified, who has demonstrated to the pride of the world that even on earth nothing is more powerful than divine humility.[45] The only "Christian Empire" that Augustine ever speaks of is the domination of the earth by Christianity, or rather by Christ the Emperor, and this is something that came about "not through the violence of bellicose struggle but through the power of unconquerable truth."[46]

And so the faith which converted the emperors becomes the faith of the emperors. As an interpretation of the past, all of this is unexceptionable. But how adequate is it in shaping a policy for the future? Everything is allowed to rest upon the slender reed of the personalities of the emperors.

Augustine, not having the benefit of fifteen more centuries' experience with Christian rulers and politicians, may be excused a certain naiveté. And there are reasons for the approach that he took. The Empire had always been to a great extent a government by men rather than laws, its policies shifting drastically as emperors changed, and after the third century it was increasingly so. Augustine quite naturally thought of government more in personal than in institutional terms. And this fitted neatly with the theory of the relation of Church and Empire that was brought to full formulation and execution by Ambrose, the theory that a Christian emperor is without question a son of the Church like all his brethren, obligated to obey the will of God as interpreted to him by that Church, and, if it comes to a conflict, liable to its discipline. Although it had the advantage of asserting the freedom of the Church from the Empire (something that was not always self-evident during the fourth century), this theory, as we can now see, made two fateful assumptions. The one was that government (which in effect means the emperor) has jurisdiction in matters of religion, even though it may look to the advice of the Church. The other was that governmental authority, when vested in believers, can be brought under the control of their personal beliefs and of their Church.[47] On these two assumptions hang many of the later struggles between Church and State in the West.

The duel with the pagans was at least straightforward and clean, as such things go. Idolatry was impiety under the law of both reason and revelation, and the emperor had authority to prohibit it as a crime and punish violations. The issues become murkier and the resolution more sinister after 404, following the imperial measures not against the pagans but the Donatists. There is an important legal distinction here. The pagans were punished for the crime of impiety or sacrilege, while the Donatists were "coerced" (and this is a technical legal term for measures taken under the police power not to punish crimes but to compel someone to take affirmative action). Ironically, this is probably the same legal procedure as that under which the Christians had earlier been persecuted by the Empire; and just as the proconsuls

21

had sought conversion rather than punishment and used force chiefly to shake them from their obstinacy, now the Christian governors sought the correction of the Donatists in the same way. Augustine tells us that he was originally reluctant to see coercion used against the Donatists, but that he was persuaded by the actual results of the imperial legislation of 404 and by the gratitude expressed personally by former Donatists who had become reconciled with the Catholic Church.[48]

His rationale was that one must restrain one's enemy when he is delirious and in danger of destroying himself. Even though it may appear to be mere persecution, the motives are different, and the deserts of those who suffer are different. Therefore when the good coerce the evil it is a work of love toward their enemies, an expression of concern for their correction and salvation.[49] The argument was such a fruitful one that he did not limit it to the Donatist question, but applied it to the pagans as well. When a leading citizen of Calama wrote asking clemency for pagan rioters, painting a picture of innocent persons being dragged to questioning under torture, Augustine waved off any suggestion of vindictiveness; the motive is certainly not punishment or revenge, he claimed, but only the correction of those who have done wrong.[50]

Whatever we may think of them, Augustine took his principles seriously. His correspondence is full of letters to imperial officials urging them to use gentle treatment in all matters having to do with religion. "The cause of the province is one thing, the cause of the Church is another," he said; "When you are acting, it is really the Church who acts, because you are acting on her account and as her son."[51] It is this line of thought, I suggest, that led to the patriarchal conception of government which several historians have noted in Augustine. He recommends in a letter to Marcellinus, for example, that a parental type of discipline, such as beating with rods, be used, commenting that this is a sentence often imposed in the bishops' courts.[52] The whole world was being brought under tutelage.

This paternalistic and inevitably repressive approach to politics remained. Even during the years when he was writing the first ten books of *The City of God*, which seem to express disillusionment with the possibilities of political life, Augustine, if anything, tightened the *compelle intrare* argument even more.[53] In the intoxication of a world rapidly becoming Christian and Catholic, Augustine yielded to the temptation to supplement the work of the divine Word, speaking through reason and revelation, with the command of the Emperor, and the work of the Spirit, moving within the heart, with the solicitous care of the Church. He considered it a matter of divine right, therefore, that the Empire, heeding the testimony of the Church, should both punish those who offend the true God through idolatry and coerce those who, in spite of professing Christ and being baptized, remain outside the unity of the Church.

Relief from this stifling atmosphere of righteousness and love was afforded by the scattered signs

23

that everything was not flourishing under the Christian emperors. Augustine and his correspondents became aware of barbarian incursions in Egypt and in other parts of the Empire. These things should arouse sorrow, but not wonder, he says. They also have been foretold. Who should be surprised if the world is beaten like a disobedient servant? People remark on the rapidity with which the gospel has been believed, but not so often on the perversity with which it is still despised. There are success stories, to be sure—a miracle delivered the three youths from the fiery furnace, in order that the king might be converted to the true God; but there was no such miraculous deliverance in the case of the Jewish martyrs who were put to death under Antiochus Epiphanes, to his condemnation.[54] This latter possibility must still be taken seriously, then, and in the last and greatest of his apologetic works, *The City of God*, he exerted his efforts once more toward differentiating the kingdom of Christ from the political kingdom.

III. Defense of the City of God

Augustine says that *The City of God* was occasioned by the sack of Rome by the Goths in 410, and that he wrote it, "glowing with zeal for the house of God," as a refutation of the pagan critics and a demonstration and defense of the Christian religion.[55]

It was once more a time for defense. The mood of exultation over "Christian times" was gone. Now they had become questionable, the very focus of debate, and the term was to be found more often in the mouths of taunting pagans or despairing Christians.[56] Augustine acknowledges the problem, and it is evident that he draws back and begins loosening the affective bonds that tie him to the external condition of his society. Perhaps all things will perish in Christian times. But God did not promise that these things would remain—he promised eternal things, which cannot be lost.[57] Perhaps Rome did fall. But a city consists not of its walls and houses, but of its citizens; the integrity of their mores can be preserved in the midst of poverty, and their minds can fall in ruin in the midst of wealth.[58] Perhaps some of the citizens of Rome did perish. But they did not really perish but only migrated to a better place if they loved God.[59]

Augustine finds, therefore, that he must add to the traditional apologetic themes a new one, a defense of Christian times in the light of the disasters that have occurred, not only under the Christian emperors (though that by itself might have been bad enough) but also after the worship of the traditional deities was prohibited.[60] His discomfiture places him in a situation more like our own, as we look back over the Christian centuries under the cold light cast by Voltaire and Gibbon. Augustine backs off, as we must, in the face of events that make Christian claims more problematical. He finds it necessary to begin again and build an argument that is complete both in its destruction

25

of the opposing position and in its demonstration of his own. Therefore the first ten books can be viewed as a systematic assault on the presuppositions of classical politics and religion, the last twelve as a presentation of the Christian understanding of human life.[61]

The disasters around 410 caused Augustine to change not so much his principles as the context in which they are interpreted. Most of the details in *The City of God* are to be found in earlier works as well, and usually with the same sense. What is different is the framework within which they find their place. To take perhaps the major example, the theme of the two metaphorical cities, the two moral societies constituted by opposed orientations in life, had long been present in Augustine's thought; and the problem of Church and Empire had also been present. But the two pairs of concepts had not been brought into relationship with each other. Now Church and Empire are taken up into the other dimension of the two metaphorical cities where ultimate issues are being decided, though without ceasing to remain themselves, in their own empirical reality.[62]

In the prologue Augustine sets as his theme the city of God, and, directly confronting the task of political apologetics, proposes to defend it through contrast with the proud city of Rome, which is, at least at the beginning, what Augustine means by the "earthly city."[63] In one sense the work is a call to decide between these two cities, and there is constant comparison between them, in the first part as well as the second. But there cannot be mere differentiation and opposition. In order to decide between them it is necessary to gain some vantage point above them, so that judgments can be made. What I suggest—though perhaps it can be proved more easily from Augustine's other, more terse and occasional writings in political apologetics than from *The City of God*—is that the point of contact between the two alien cities is the notion of "eternal law," already made venerable by classical philosophy and carried over into medieval thought by the mediation of Augustine and others. With this he will refute, from the philosophers themselves, the traditional system of politics and religion; and with it he will also demonstrate why it is that the Christian Church must speak to *all* aspects of life, though always in a religious rather than a political vein, and laying them under claim not in her own behalf but in God's.[64]

Despite his bitter condemnation of the realities of human life, Augustine never ceased to hold an absolute ideal before it, for the eternal law remains in force, indeed, it is being proclaimed once again in the churches throughout the world. Therefore his reaction to the critics of Christian times is never a purely defensive one, for he assumes that the eternal law of which the philosophers were dimly aware is the same law that is being put into effect through the proclamation of the gospel.[65] And it is not only right; it is also expedient. Augustine asserts, without qualification, that the message proclaimed by the churches, far from being contrary to the public good, is rather its guarantee (*salus rei publicae*).[66] He paints an ideal possibility: if all —rulers and subjects, old and young—were to observe these precepts, then there would be a common life of unparalleled splendor, with concord and righteousness on earth, and hope of eternal happiness in the divine city.[67] Passages like these tend to support the contention of those who see in Augustine the seeds of the medieval view that the law of God ought to rule over all of life—though it is difficult to find any confirmation in Augustine's own writings for the claim that the *Church* ought to exercise this rule.[68]

Still, we should not mistake his picture of it. The perfection he has in mind has to do primarily with the inward posture of the heart, not with external actions; its splendor is that of virtue. It is even rather ascetic, for it requires that all temporal things be used properly, with reference to God, and not be sought and enjoyed for their own sake.[69] The eternal law is really quite simple—it is the love of God and of one's neighbor in God.

This is law in a different and quite unaccustomed sense. It cannot be mistaken for political law; it is primarily religious and moral. And there is little danger that law, when it has this character, will become abstract and formal; it has the whole self for its content, and its legal obligation cannot be divorced from its source and focus in God himself.[70]

How this can be the eternal law of which the philosophers had some inkling, yet which they never fully understood, is explained if we follow the steps in Augustine's reasoning. The eternal law is variously stated, sometimes in terms of the classic definition of justice—"giving to each what is his own," or "giving to each his rights"[71] —and sometimes in a fuller way that summarizes the entire providential ordering of the world—"the law which commands the preservation of natural order and forbids its disturbance."[72] Thus Augustine picks up the classical notion of natural law. But he then transforms it into a law of personal relations. In the "natural order" that is involved here we should not stress nature, which may connote inevitability, so much as order, the appropriate relation between natures, for the question is what is appropriate to a free and rational being like man, and the answer is the subordination of oneself to God and the ordering of all other relations "in God."[73]

Consequently the only truly just society is the city of God, because it alone serves God and takes him as its "common good." It is also the only truly equitable and secure and happy society, for the unique characteristic of spiritual possession, as Augustine often notes, is that all can share the same object without rivalry and without diminution.[74] We should not be surprised, then, to find Augustine taking Cicero's definition of civil society and radicalizing it in order to show that the only true society is the city of God. He does this twice, and with enough suspense and solemnity to show that he intended it to be a dramatic climax in which he scores a decisive point against his opponents. If there is civil society only where there is mutual acknowledgment of right (*ius*), and if this is based only on justice (*iustitia*), and if justice is the virtue of giving to each—and especially to God—his due, then the conclusion follows inevitably.[75]

I hope I have shown that Augustine did have a picture of the perfect society, sketched out from eternity in the divine mind and at least glimpsed by the philosophers. This perfect society, in which the external is always controlled by conscious resolve and there is harmony between the individual and the social, has tantalizing similarities with Rousseau's general will, or Hegel's state, or Marx's fully human society—or rather they are politicized versions of an originally religious vision. What they have in common is that an ideal stands over the deficient human realities, both to judge them and to draw them on toward better achievements which are to be enacted in the medium of human existence. The difference, of course, is that Augustine strips away all natural and even historical inevitability and sees the realization of the ideal as being pervaded with contingency, because of both the freedom of the will and, beyond that, the freedom of divine grace; for without grace, and without response to grace, the ideal would remain an empty command, followed out at best by a perverse imitation of God. That is why Augustine concerns himself with the original state of angels and men, and devotes so much attention to the actual history of the two cities, and stakes so much upon demonstrating the need for a "way" which will meet the human race within the realm of its own experience.[76]

For the eternal law is not reflected automatically in a correct ordering of human life; it calls upon human wills, and their response is the either/or which shapes the two metaphorical cities: either love of God, even to the contempt of self, or love of self, even to the contempt of God.[77] Because of the solidarity of the human race, sin even means that all are born first into the earthly city, and only then are reborn into the heavenly city through grace.[78] But the two cities are not equal in strength —it is not a Zoroastrian struggle between two eternal principles. Augustine stresses the weakness and deficiency of evil, its parasitism on the goodness of creation. And especially in the case of human history, we need to remind ourselves that his usual designation is not "city of the devil" but "earthly city," and he describes it as those who live, not "according to nothingness" or "according to Satan," but "according to the flesh" or "according to man." His best definition of the earthly city is to be found well along in *The City of God*, where he speaks of "the earthborn city, the society of men living according to man, under the domination of the rebel angels." Its damnation is not yet definitive, and its possibilities for good are not entirely lost.[79]

Augustine believes Paul when he says (Romans 2, 14) that the Gentiles do by nature the works of the law written in their hearts. He understands this to mean that an awareness of the eternal law,

31

inscribed on their hearts by the divine Word, is never effaced, and they even do those things that the law commands.[80] And although Augustine often speaks of earthly societies, and of Rome in particular, with a pitiless tone of denunciation that continues to surprise and fascinate, we cannot help but notice that he also ascribes to them, at least to Rome, a degree of justice and virtue, though he qualifies such statements by contrasting these with *true* justice or *true* virtue.[81] And God does not let these achievements go unrecognized. Even though they cannot inherit eternal life, still "they have their reward" (Matthew 6, 2), for they have been given the temporal glory of a vast empire. All that was needed to bring the civic virtues of the Romans to their proper fulfillment was their conversion to the worship of the true God. Indeed, Augustine even sees many intimations in their history that the Romans sensed that their own gods were not worthy of them. Why did they prohibit lampooning a public figure on the stage but not object to the same treatment of their gods, why did they bar actors from public honors even though they counted the theater as part of the honor due to the gods, except that they knew that these gods were not their equal?[82]

There has been much debate over the extent to which Augustine ascribed an authentic justice to human societies, with the answers ranging from strongly pessimistic to strongly affirmative views of that possibility. We will do better if we recognize that eternal law, as he understands it, can apply

32

quite flexibly to all circumstances. If human wills do not respond to the law's command to observe the right ordering of man to God, then the law takes the form of judgment, letting the consequences of sin follow, so that, with a kind of moral physics, they will still find their appropriate "level" in the total order of things.[83] It is in this connection that Augustine argues that many of the social structures with which we live—indeed, all of those that are external, institutional, and coercive rather than spontaneous and communal—are what we deserve because of our own sinful tendencies, either as a kind of symbolization of the condition all of us are in (and this seems to be his opinion of slavery) or, more often, as a control upon sin or even a corrective to it (this is the role of government in his view). Not all of these structures are just—Augustine's redefinition of civil society was devised for the purpose of showing that concord and order may be had *without* justice—but even these are imposed "justly" by divine providence. And justice itself can be applied in the alien medium of external interactions, not as such, not as the virtue, the inward orientation, that alone deserves the name of justice, but in human laws and institutions that are "just" to a certain degree.[84]

Now in all of this we can see Augustine adopting a strategy for apologetics, and perhaps even more important, a strategy for the life of the Church itself. He grants to his opponents a sense of justice, he grants that their laws and institutions have been, to some degree, just, he grants that their

33

actions have often manifested a heroic virtue. The members of the city of God can share in these things with them, taking as their policy the advice of Jeremiah to the exiles in Babylon (Jeremiah 29) to build houses and marry and beget children, and to seek the temporal peace of Babylon.[85] Augustine can be generous, because he reserves the fatal blow for another point. What counts ultimately is not external justice or civic virtue but the relation of the heart to God and one's fellows. Whatever coalitions may be formed in public or private life, whatever mutual esteem there may be, whatever one's physical relationship to the Church may be, the distinction between act and motivation, between the values that are willed and the ultimate value for whose sake they are willed, keeps reopening the question to which city one belongs, which of the two loves is predominant.

But the question does not end there, for the inward orientation expresses itself in adherence to one or the other of the two communities as historical movements. To be sure, we are born into the earthly city and continue to share its life; the two cities are inseparably tangled together as long as earthly conditions last; the city of God cannot be identified in any simple sense with the Church. Nevertheless adherence to the Church is, under normal conditions, a prerequisite to being a member of the city of God, or rather that part of it which now wanders like a stranger or resident alien (*peregrinus*) on earth.[86]

34

And we should not suppose, merely on the strength of those many passages in which Augustine takes a detached attitude toward earthly gain or loss, that he thinks the Church should take a passive stance toward temporal affairs, looking up to the heavens. The city of God which he is championing is a historical movement, the same one whose heritage can be traced throughout human time and which has recently conquered an Empire through its willingness to confront its religious policies and political claims openly. The members of that city cannot fail to be an unsettling and reconstructive force in their world. Notice what Augustine does in book XIX, even while he is gratefully accepting the peace of Babylon, affirming its multiplicity of mores, laws, and institutions, and admitting the propriety of slavery and coercive government as consequences of sin. The master and the ruler, he says, are to care for those they seem to command, and even to serve them, just as the office of bishop involves "a work, not an honor." And over it all there hovers the reminder that the city of God, which calls citizens out of all nations, accepting their diversity of customs, *cannot* share their view of man's ultimate loyalties and is willing to dissent and risk their hatred; for it must follow the criterion enunciated in books IX and X that no principle of mediation can be acknowledged, whether in heaven or on earth, which does not bring all into direct encounter with God on terms of a fundamental equality. In the midst of all these tensions, he says, whenever the city of

God will let its social relationships be controlled and transformed by the law of love, it is already enjoying the peace of God's city, though more in hope than in reality.[87]

As he comes toward the close of his defense of the city of God and looks toward the earthly future, Augustine returns to a version of "historical" apologetics from the character of Christian existence, but it is chastened now, in the manner of Paul, with a constant sense of the tension between "now" and "later," between "hope" and "reality." Believers, he says, have even more difficulties than others: in their constant warfare against temptation and struggle against their own vices they are never able to rest. The peace they can now attain consists more in consolation than in positive enjoyment; their righteousness consists more in the remission of sins than in the perfecting of virtue.[88] The millenium, during which believers rule with Christ, is now equated with the present period when the tares grow in the midst of the wheat and even the elect must live in constant dependence on the forgiveness of God; and the thousand-year reign even includes the unleashing of Satan as a final test of the steadfastness of the saints.[89] This is an apologetics in which the conclusion can scarcely be read off directly from the phenomena; it flourishes on paradox, finding victory in the midst of struggle, strength in weakness, the seeds of growth in the blood of the martyrs, as though to say that the apologetic task reaches its end not in direct knowledge or even in correct judgment but in decision whether or not to join in the same uncertain battle, amid the same contradictions.

In the fashion of a Tertullian (or a Paul), he defiantly seizes upon the alleged incredibility of Christian belief (specifically here the resurrection of Christ). If this is incredible, he says, then it is also incredible that the whole world should have believed such an incredible thing, and it is incredible, furthermore, that the world should have been persuaded by a few simple men with no education: there are not one but *three* incredible things, then. But if we leave to one side the resurrection of Christ and the miracles of the apostles (for these, he recognizes, may be open to historical doubt), there is still the "one great miracle" that, in enlightened times, when people are sophisticated about what is possible and impossible, the whole world has believed, even without seeing miracles, and in the midst of persecution and martyrdom, a faith that seemed incredible. Therefore this faith is *not* incredible, at least in the sense that it is in fact believed and preached throughout the world; if it seemed incredible at first, that is now shown to have been because it was new and unaccustomed, not because it was incredible and contrary to reason.[90]

And yet, is this one great miracle of universal belief as clear a sign as one might suppose? Is it really so obvious that anyone who still asks for prodigies in order that he might believe is himself a great prodigy, since he does not believe when the whole world believes? Is this faith which at

37

first was so new and unaccustomed that miracles had to be performed in order to break through the accumulated web of habitual expectations, now so familiar that it can be believed without difficulty? This *could* be the case. But Augustine seems to share in the dilemma he had been preparing for the doubting philosophers: either faith in an incredible event which was not witnessed has been caused by other incredible things which both occurred and were witnessed; or else this event was so credible that it needed no miracles at all in proof of it. The first of these alternatives, he says, was actually the case at the beginning, for faith in the resurrection was evoked by the miracles of the apostles. Is it now sufficient merely to rely upon the multitude of those who believe as contemporary proof of that faith?[91]

And so the same Augustine who through most of his career had taken a reserved attitude toward claims of contemporary miracles now evinces a sudden interest in them (most of them associated with relics of St. Stephen, brought to Africa in 418 and to Hippo in 424). He goes into the subject with the thoroughness of an intellectual, having documents drawn up and certified so that the full narrative could be read in the church soon after the event and reread on the martyrs' days as the years went on. Miracles are still being wrought, he asserts, and they are to be interpreted as external signs of divine approval of the martyrs themselves and of the faith for which they showed such constancy.[92]

The center of gravity in this argument, it will be noted, as in all other arguments from miracle, or from prophecy, or from the expansion of the Church, is the *faith*, the *proclamation*, that is confirmed by them. But why is it that miracles wrought by the *martyrs* are the decisive contemporary proof of this faith? Buried in the midst of the discussion, like a concealed middle term, is the suggestion that the martyrs themselves are a sign confirming the faith, with or without the miracles that come later, because this faith, this proclamation, was the basis of their steadfastness.[93] Here, I submit, we find Augustine's last word on the demonstration of the Spirit and of power, going deeper than any outward wonders, more integrally related to the faith that is being presented, more capable of speaking with persuasive authority, more satisfactory than the mere phenomenon of geographical expanse to a theologian who is becoming increasingly aware of the tensions and struggles of Christian existence, more perfectly in the spirit of Paul.

We have been able to see how seriously Augustine took the apologetic task, and we have observed him wrestling with it in the face of several quite different challenges. But we should ask ourselves at the end what can be said in a more general way about his strategy as an apologist.

First, he knows, of course, that he must look for a point of contact with his partners in debate, try to find which of their insights and aspirations can be shared, and address them, if not always with gentleness, at least with the willingness to engage them out in the open.

Then he tries, where he can, to show how the Christian faith makes it possible for those insights and aspirations to be better understood and, even more important, to be put into effect. He places much weight on its results, whether in private or in public life, in religion or in politics. And if one of the burdens of apologetics is to show that the Christian faith does make a difference, then the burden of the Church is to make good that claim by *exhibiting* the difference, so that it can speak with genuine authority.

But he is sometimes forced, whether by controversy or by plain honesty, to recognize that the Christian phenomenon may not always be a straightforward confirmation of Christian claims. Under those circumstances it seems to be necessary to move beyond the "Christian phenomenon," an observable state of affairs which can somehow justify itself, to "Christian existence," an inward posture that must finally seek its justification from God alone, if not through the whirlwind of prophecy or the storm of miracle, then through the still voice of grace and promise; and this Christian existence can be, even then, a human sign of confirmation if it is received with faith and hope.

ABBREVIATIONS USED IN NOTES

AM	*Augustinus Magister. Actes du Congrès international augustinien* (3 vols., Paris 1954)
Archives	*Archives d'histoire doctrinale et littéraire du moyen âge* (Paris)
Augustinus	*Augustinus. Strenas Augustinianas P. Victorino Capánaga oblatas* (Madrid, vol. I 1967, vol. II 1968)
DTC	*Dictionnaire de théologie catholique* (Paris)
JRS	*Journal of Roman Studies* (London)
RA	*Recherches augustiniennes* (Paris)
REA	*Revue des études augustiniennes* (Paris)
TLZ	*Theologische Literaturzeitung* (Leipzig)
VC	*Vigiliae Christianae* (Amsterdam)
ZKG	*Zeitschrift für Kirchengeschichte* (Gotha, Stuttgart)

NOTES

1. Origen, *Contra Celsum,* Translated with an Introduction and Notes by Henry Chadwick (2nd ed. Cambridge 1965) 8.

The "demonstration of the Spirit and of power" (I Cor. 2.4) is an important theme throughout the work, and in both I.2 and VI.2 (the major statements) it is set in contrast to the dialectical arguments of the philosophers (cf. also *De principiis* IV.1.7, with its almost identical formulation). It is to be noted that Celsus himself makes a similar point by contrasting mere "talk" with "proofs in actual achievements" (oracles and miracles) as alternative ways of deciding which religious option is nearer the truth and more efficacious (quoted in VIII.48).

The notion that "traces" (ἴχνη, *vestigia*) of the powers manifested in Christ and the apostles are still preserved is found frequently in *C. Cels.*: cf. I.46 ("traces of the same Holy Spirit" continue when Christians exorcise daemons, heal diseases, and see visions of the future), VII.8 ("signs" and "traces" of the Holy Spirit), and especially II.8 ("traces are to be found to some extent among Christians, and sometimes they are even greater" [John 14.12]). In II.48 it is explained how these later miracles are even greater: they consist in opening the eyes of those who are *inwardly* blind, and making those who are *inwardly* lame leap as a hart.

2. *Lessing's Theological Writings,* Selections in Translation with an Introductory Essay by Henry Chadwick (Stanford 1957) 51-56. Cf. the editor's comments (30-49).

It is no accident that Chadwick translated both Origen and Lessing. See his article, 'The Evidences of Christianity in the Apologetic of Origen,' *Studia Patristica* 2 (= *Texte und Untersuchungen* 64, Berlin 1957) 331-39, in which he discusses Origen as a prime architect of the three "historical" arguments—from prophecy, miracle, and the expansion and unity of the Church— but also a thoughtful critic of them, and notes some continuities between Origen and modern thought. Mention should also be made of his *Early Christian Thought and the Classical Tradition: Studies in Justin, Clement, and Origen* (Oxford 1966).

3. One of the characteristics of modern apologetics has been its interest, on one side, in human subjectivity and its strivings, and, on the other, in the Christian faith or the Church as the resolution of these strivings. Most of the discussion has centered upon the "motives of credibility," that is, those human tendencies and those experienced facts that lead first to the judgment that the Christian faith is "credible," then to the judgment that it is "credentible" (something one ought to believe), and finally to the act of faith itself. Apologetics thus leads toward faith, as two classic texts suggest (Augustine, *De praed. sanct.* 2.5: "No one believes something unless he has first thought of it as something that ought to be believed," and Thomas Aquinas, *S.T.* II-II q. 1 a. 4 ad 2: "He who believes . . . would not have believed unless he had seen these things as something that ought to be believed, either because of the evidence of signs or because of other factors of that sort," with the further explanation (ibid., ad 3), "The light of faith is what makes these things to be seen [as something to be believed]"). In the more traditional apologetics there was a reliance on argumentation, especially upon demonstration of the fact of revelation through the three great "historical" proofs. In the newer kind of apologetics represented by many twentieth-century figures, by contrast, an attempt is made to exhibit the character of Christian existence, on the assumption that life, not argument, is most likely to arouse the disposition to believe. Consequently apologetics has also moved closer to two other disciplines, the analysis of the act of faith (its "formal object," its ultimate motive, its preconditions) and "fundamental theology" (the examination of the "foundations" of theology in revelation

43

and faith). For a summary of the older discussion, see A. Gardeil, 'Crédibilité,' DTC III.2 cols. 2201-2310; for the twentieth-century developments, Roger Aubert, *Le problème de l'acte de foi* (3rd ed. Louvain 1958); for the most recent ferment, Johannes B. Metz (ed.), *The Development of Fundamental Theology* (Concilium 46, New York 1969). The observable data that are the "motives of credibility" are always kept distinct from the internal apprehension that what has been heard ought to be believed because of the authority of God the Revealer; but the emphasis can be either upon their logical difference or their practical continuity, and experience seems to suggest that the former approach, precisely because of the care and objectivity with which its arguments are drawn, runs the risk of distancing itself from those who are being addressed, while the latter, relying not on "inference" from "facts" but upon the transparent witness of Christian existence, is able to exhibit it as a living invitation to join in that same heritage.

4. Origen acknowledges that the disciples were deficient in literary style, in dialectic and rhetoric, and in the ability to construct an ordered narrative (*C. Cels.* I.62, III.39 and 48). He even agrees with the prejudices of the critics, suggesting that it is not plausible that unlettered men should be bold enough to proclaim the gospel and have such sudden success except because they relied upon divine power (VIII.47).

The proof from conviction is found in II.10 and 56, III.3, and VII.7 (cf. also *De princ.* IV.1.5).

Even the priests of the mysteries, Origen acknowledges, teach about rewards and punishments in the next life, but the question is who "is able to make the people who hear what they say live as though these things were real" (VIII.48). Similarly the philosophers do not have the power to convert and strengthen others (VI.2). By contrast, Jesus' power consisted in both words and facts, and even his word was "with power" (II.73; cf. I.30-31); and in later times his words and works convert both the simple and the intelligent (VII.54).

The philosophers, who claim to follow reason and shun mere custom, give in to custom when it comes to worship (V.35). Despite their impressive teachings they fall down to idols and daemons, while the lowliest Jew looks only to the supreme God (V.43; VII.46). The Peripatetics and the followers of Democritus and Epicurus, who are so proud of their careful inquiries into the nature of things, still accomodate to the multitude by pretending to pray to images (VII.66; cf. *Exhortation to Martyrdom* 6). Not even Socrates and Plato escape condemnation, for they both succumbed to idolatry (VI.3-5). Socrates was called "wiser than all men" by the Pythian oracle—but this was probably because of the sacrifices he had brought to the daemon (VII.6). "Though what Plato said was true, it did not help his readers toward a true religion, nor even Plato himself" (VI.5; cf. VI.17). And some of the philosophers are even attracted by magic and commerce with the daemons, especially those who take an interest in the "magician and philosopher" Apollonius of Tyana (VI.41).

5. The philosophers, who ought to follow reason rather than national custom, fail to do this when it comes to worship (V.35). Lawgivers and philosophers have often seen it as desirable to propagate more rational laws and teachings among nations other than their own, but they have not even attempted to do so, knowing that they had little chance of success. But thousands of "zealots" have abandoned their "ancestral laws and legal gods" to follow Moses and Christ, though they are hated and even in danger of death (*De princ.* IV.1.1). This is a rational and spiritual worship, suited to the entire human race (*C. Cels.* III.40 and 81; IV.26 and 32). Consequently Origen can answer without flinching Celsus' question where the Christians came from and who gave them their traditional laws (q. in V.33), for the admits that the Christians are a new people, "born in an instant" (VIII.43)— indeed, he says in another work, the Christians are a "non-people" (Deut. 32.21), since they were never an integral nation but rather have been gathered here and there from all the peoples (*Hom. I in Ps. 36* [*PG* 12.155]).

On the improvement of morals (ἐπιστροφή, βελτίωσις, ἐπανορθώσις ἠθῶν) see especially *C. Cels.* I.43; also, in answer to Celsus' accusation (III.16-18 and IV.10) that the Christians win and sustain conviction by using scare tactics and making unsubstantiated claims, just like the popular religions, the reply that the Christians can give reasons, and they are good reasons: the

45

acts and the aims that are proclaimed are worthy of God, and the evidence is in the lives of men (III.28, 31, 33, 42; V.3; VII.6).

This importance of this last defense will be evident when one glances at the anti-Christian literature of the early centuries. Pliny, in his letter to Trajan, speaks of Christianity as a depraved superstition. Epictetus (*Diss.* IV.7.6) says that the Galilaeans suffer fearlessly, but it is from madness or habit and they cannot profit from reasonable demonstration; Marcus Aurelius (*Med.* XI.3.2) similarly accounts for their bravery as παράταξις—perhaps perversity or contrariety, perhaps the blind fanaticism or discipline of an army.

6. Possidius, in his *Indiculus* of Augustine's works (PL 45.5) lists under works *contra paganos* the following:

> *De Academicis* (or *Contra Academicos*)
> *De ordine*
> *De utilitate credendi*
> *De vera religione*
> *De animae immortalitate*
> A number of questions in *De diversis quaestionibus 83*
> *De consensu evangelistarum*
> *Quaestiones contra Porphyrium expositae sex* (Ep. 102)
> *De divinatione daemonum*
> *De civitate Dei*

If we reflect on the various apologetic themes in Augustine's writings, we come up with a list that includes at least the following:

> The possibility of certain knowledge (Cassiciacum dialogues, especially C. *Acad.* III)
> The necessity of belief based on authority (Cassiciacum dialogues; *De vera religione; De utilitate credendi; De fide rerum quae non videntur*)
> Exhortations to conversion (*De vera religione, De civitate Dei*)
> Defense of Christian beliefs against Manichaean and pagan criticisms (*De libero arbitrio*; Ep. 102; *De civitate Dei*)
> Defense of the Scriptures against Manichaean and pagan criticisms (*De Genesi contra Manichaeos; Contra Faustum Manichaeum; De consensu evangelistarum; De Genesi ad litteram*)
> Defense of the Catholic Church's acquiescence in coercion (*Contra litteras Petiliani; Contra Cresconium;* Epp. 93, 105, 173, 185, etc.; *Contra Gaudentium*)

Defense of *tempora christiana* (Ep. 102; various sermons; *De civitate Dei*).

7. See especially *De Trin.* VIII.4.6-6.9, 9.13, where all authority is grounded in the divine Word as the criterion by which everything that is proposed for belief must be judged. The twin commandment of love foɪ God and one's neighbor in God is made the sum of the law, the prophets, and the gospel in numerous passages (e.g., *De doct. chr.* I.35.39-36.40; Ep. 137.5.17; *De civ. Dei* X.18 and XIX.14).

It is to be noted that Augustine almost never cites I Cor. 2.4 ("demonstration of the Spirit and of power"), probably because he understands Paul well enough to know that the apostle really placed emphasis not upon miracles and charismatic gifts but upon love, on the one side (I. Cor. 12-13), and upon walking in fear and trembling, on the other. James M. Robinson and Helmut Koester, *Trajectories through Early Christianity* (Philadelphia 1971), chs. 2 and 6, emphasize the contrast between Paul and other strands of early Christian thought, which tended to rely in a direct, undialectical way upon miracle, charisma, or wisdom.

8. Note, for example, his criticism of the common limitation of all knowledge to sense and imagination (*Conf.* III.4.8 and 6.10; V.3.3 and 10.19-20; VIII.1.2-2.3), and his refutation of the Academics' doubt that we can know anything with certitude (*C. Acad.* III; *Solil.* II).

9. See especially the Cassiciacum dialogues, *Conf.* VII, and *De civ. Dei* VIII-X. The Stoics, by contrast, are condemned as practicing "the philosophy of this world" (Col. 2.8) because they suppose that knowledge must come through sensation (*C. Acad.* III.19.42; *Conf.* III.4.8, VIII.2.3; *De civ. Dei* VIII.10-11).

10. See esp. Plotinus, *Enn. I*.6.8; in Augustine, *De ver. rel.* 3.3.; *De doct. chr.* I.4.4, 10.10-11.11; *Conf.* VII.20.26-21.27; *De Trin.* IV.15.20; *De civ. Dei* X.29. In his later writings Augustine, elaborating on the imagery, suggests that they are being preyed upon by the daemons, runaways from heaven's army, led by the devil, who is lion and serpent in one (*Conf.* VII.21.27); therefore those who wish to return to the heavenly city must, like the Magi, return by another way, where the wicked king cannot lie in wait (*De Trin.* IV.12.15). But this theme is not present until about 397,

47

when Augustine begins to manifest more concern with the pagan religions as worship of the daemons.

11. *Conf.* V.13.23. See especially Pierre Courcelle, *Recherches sur les Confessions de saint Augustin* (Paris 1950) 78-83.

12. *C. Acad.* II.2.5. I have tried to show this in *Augustine the Theologian* (London and New York 1970) 33-43.

13. *De doct. chr.* II.40.60-41.62; *Conf.* VII.9.15.

14. *Ep.* 118.3.16-21. Similarly in *De cons. ev.* I.23.35 Augustine suggests that "in Christian times" the Platonists were ashamed of the usual philosophical interpretation of Cronos as *chronos* (time), and preferred *koros-nous* or *satur-nous* (fullness of mind). Historians have often noted the increasingly religious character of middle Platonism and especially neo-Platonism, and there is still room for debate over the question to what extent it was directly influenced by competition with the Christian movement (and there was competition, as Porphyry shows), and to what extent it was only a parallel movement responding to similar cultural conditions.

15. *De ver. rel.* 2.2, 4.6-7.

16. *C. Acad.* III.19.42 (the vicissitudes of philosophy, with only a trickle of correct doctrine); *De ver. rel.* 4.6 (the timid guesses of a few); *De civ. Dei* XIII.17 ("human conjectures" as against the inspired statements of the prophets), XVIII.41 (human weakness as against divine authority), XVIII.51 (the "confusion" of philosophical opinions in Babylon as against the Church's "amazing agreement"). Olof Gigon, *Die antike Kultur und das Christentum* (Gütersloh 1966) 148-49 notes that, while a few philosophers became martyrs to their beliefs (Socrates, Anaxarchus, Cato of Utica), they were generally aware of the limits of knowledge and were not ready to die over disputed opinions.

17. Authority is set in contrast to reason or direct experience. Most often it involves testimony, given by someone who can be trusted, about things to which we have no direct access, or only imperfect access. What it gives is not knowledge in the strict sense but belief, though this belief is characterized by certitude. When it come to divine authority we are well beyond the rather external notion of testimony in the human sense (such as that of a traveler telling us about a distant part of the world, or a

48

historical document telling us about past events). It is authority in the sense of "authorship," in the way that writings from the past reveal what their author had in mind, or (in the ancient use of the term) a city and its institutions disclose the conceptions which brought it to birth. What is learned from divine authority is, on one side, God's own nature, and, on the other, the *dispensatio temporalis*, God's intentions and acts and commands throughout human history. Lacking direct access to God, Augustine argues, we must humbly follow what is given by authority as the only way of return to him (*De ver. rel.* 50, 99; *De fid. et symb.* 4.6 and 6.8; *De doct. chr.* I.34.38-35.39). The efficaciousness of authority is usually described in terms of "persuading" (*De ver. rel.* 2.2-4.7) or "moving" (*De util. cred.* 16.34) to conviction and commitment.

For a general discussion of authority and belief, see Magnus Löhrer, *Der Glaubensbegriff des hl. Augustinus in seinen ersten Schriften bis zu den Confessiones* (Einsiedeln 1955). There are some extremely useful comments in Louis de Mondadon, 'Bible et Église dans l'apologétique de saint Augustin,' *Recherches de science religieuse* 2 (1911) 558-60, and Wilhelm Kamlah, *Christentum und Geschichtlichkeit. Untersuchungen zur Entstehung des Christentums und zu Augustins "Bürgerschaft Gottes."* (2nd ed. Stuttgart and Cologne 1951) 212-14.

18. This is the case with Christ, in whom the gap between divine authority and human response was closed in such a way that, "despising all that evil men desire, suffering all that they dread, and doing all that they marvel at, he converted the human race, with the highest love and authority, to so vigorous a faith" (*De ver. rel.* 3.3); with the entire course of Christianity, in which "Christ, bringing the medicine to heal corrupt morals, through his miracles gained authority, through his authority merited faith, through faith drew together a multitude, through this multitude guaranteed permanence and antiquity, and through this permanence corroborated his religion" (*De util. cred.* 14.32); and with the Church itself, which has "an authority begun by miracles, nourished by hope, enlarged by renown, and confirmed by age" (*C. ep. Man. Fund.* 4.5).

In both the Old Testament and the New Testament, miracles and other signs are demanded of those who claim to speak in

49

behalf of God, as part of their legitimating credentials. This is also the function of the argument from prophecy. Augustine, like others before him, took up the challenge, adding to miracle and the fulfillment of prophecy the "moral miracle" of the Christian life and the expansion of the Church. Throughout most of his career he felt that the age of dramatic miracles belonged to the past, as part of the inital impetus given to faith, and that its value as a sign was replaced in later times by the expanse and unity of the Christian Church (*De ver. rel.* 24.47; *De util. cred.* 16.34-17.35; and still in *De civ. Dei* XII.5).

19. *De util. cred.* 14.31, 17.35.

20. *C. ep. Man. Fund.* 5.6.

21. The autobiographical argument makes repeated mention of the numerous "bonds" which "hold" him to the Cathlolic Church (*C. ep. Man. Fund.* 4.5), so that he cannot really give credence to any alternatives. But if they do insist on mentioning the gospels (and Mani claimed to be an apostle of Jesus Christ), then he poses a dilemma: If they can show him anything in the gospels that speaks openly of Mani's apostleship, they will weaken Catholic authority in his mind—but if that authority is weakened, then he can no longer believe in the gospels at all, since it was through it that he believed in them, and he cannot continue to believe what he believed through falsehood (ibid. 5.6).

22. *De util. cred.* 17.35.

23. *De ver. rel.* 4.6; *De util. cred.* 16.34; *C. ep. Man. Fund.* 4.5.

24. *De util. cred.* 17.35; *C. ep. Man. Fund.* 4.5.

25. *De ver. rel.* 3.5; *De util. cred.* 14.31.

26. Apologetic writings during this period (397-410) include:
Contra Faustum Manichaeum (398-99), an answer to Manichaean attacks on the Old Testament as contrary to the New;

De consensu evangelistarum (400), a work undertaken because of pagan criticisms of the gospels, ultimately drawn from Porphyry, not only questioning their consistency and veracity (these are answered in books II-IV) but even claiming Jesus for themselves as one who, far from opposing the gods or daemons, paid honor to them (and this question occupies book I);

50

Ep. 102 to Deogratias or *Quaestiones contra Porphyrium expositae sex* (406 or soon after), a reply to six questions derived, once again, from Porphyry's criticisms of Christianity;

Ep. 91 to Nectarius (408), following a pagan riot in Calama which lasted for several days and resulted in numerous Christian deaths;

Ep. 104 to Nectarius (409), probably written after Possidius, the bishop of Calama, went to the imperial court to ask for sanctions against the pagan populace;

Ep. 232 to the people of Madaura (date uncertain);

Epp. 233-35 (date uncertain).

I have tried to trace Augustine's new concern with Porphyry during this period in *Augustine the Theologian* 237-58, suggesting that it resulted either from an encounter with another work of Porphyry's (perhaps the *Philosophy from Oracles*) or, if he had known it earlier, from some new feature of contemporary debate which placed it in a more dangerous light. Either way, the basic cause could be a resurgence of pagan propaganda as a last resistance movement against Theodosius' suppression of the cults. Another possible factor, much more problematical, is a lost work by Ambrose entitled *De philosophia contra Platonem* or *contra Platonicos*, which Augustine mentions in Ep. 31 to Paulinus of Nola, written in 395-96. Unfortunately little is known about this work; the only extensive quotation is found in *C. Jul. Pel.* II.7.19-20, where Platonist doctrine is contradicted from Plato's *Timaeus* in a way that bears some similarities with Augustine's own method of disputing with Porphyry.

For the controversy between pagans and Christians at the end of the fourth century, see especially Herbert Bloch, 'The Pagan Revival in the West at the End of the Fourth Century,' in Arnaldo Momigliano (ed.), *The Conflict between Paganism and Christianity in the Fourth Century* (Oxford 1963) 193-218, and, for more specialized aspects, studies such as Ronald Syme, *Ammianus and the Historia Augusta* (Oxford 1968) and Alan Cameron, 'The Date and Identity of Macrobius,' JRS 56 (1966) 25-38.

Augustine's observations on the diminishing numbers of pagans begin after the suppression of the sacrifices in 399 (esp. *De cons. ev.* I.7.10 and 27.42-28.43).

51

It is difficult to know when Augustine is concerned with survivals of popular religion in his own day and when with a paganism met through writings from an earlier time. Sister Mary Daniel Madden, *The Pagan Divinities and Their Worship as Depicted in the Works of Saint Augustine Exclusive of the City of God* (Catholic University of America Patristic Studies 24, Washington 1930), thinks that most of the references to contemporary paganism occur in works other than *The City of God*, and she collects and classifies them. Frederik Van der Meer, *Augustine the Bishop: Religion and Society at the Dawn of the Middle Ages*, translated by Brian Battershaw and G. R. Lamb (New York 1961) chs. 3 and 4, draws together many comments on paganism and its survivals from Augustine's letters and sermons. André Mandouze, 'Saint Augustin et la religion romaine," RA 1 (1958) 187-223, has extensive comments on both these earlier studies, but his chief concern is to characterize Augustine's own attitude toward paganism.

27. This theme is already sounded in the early Cassiciacum dialogues (the opposition of *superbia* and *clementia*), but it becomes a regular part of his depiction of the philosophers only later (*Conf.* VII.9.14, 20.26, 21.27; *De Trin.* IV.15.20; *De civ. Dei* X).

28. In earlier writings Augustine mentions only briefly that, while many of the Platonists have turned to Christianity, some worshiped daemons (*De ver. rel.* 4.7). The theme of deception by the daemons begins to come out more sharply in *De doct. chr.* II.23.35-36 and 40.60. It is developed fully in *Conf.* X.42.67 and *De cons. ev.* I.35.53, both of which passages bear the marks of being an answer to Porphyry's theory of mediation. The answer is repeated in *De civ. Dei* IX.15 and X.27-29 with direct reference to Porphyry.

29. The philosophers whom Augustine expecially criticizes are Varro, Apuleius, and Porphyry. Varro took the Stoic view that all the gods are merely parts or aspects of the one God who animates the world. Apuleius and Porphyry, as Platonists, acknowledged a multiplicity of celestial "gods" and intermediate "daemons," and they saw some value in cultivating them all, either as possible mediators leading toward the supreme God or, in the case of evil

daemons, as powers who must at least be placated or warded off in order to continue one's journey toward the celestial gods.

30. *De civ. Dei* X.32. Cf. the early exchange of correspondence with Maximus of Madaura (Epp. 16-17, about 390), in which Maximus affirms, in Stoic fashion, that there is one surpreme God whose powers are diffused throughout the universe, and who is worshiped under many names (since we are ignorant of his true name) and in many cults, which approach him through his different parts; and also the exchange with Longinianus (Epp. 233-35, date uncertain), in which Longinianus suggests that from time immemorial there have been many revelations from the gods—through Socrates, the prophets, the Orphics, Hermes Trismegistus, and others—and that there are many ancient rites for purifying the soul. The same argument is used in Symmachus' appeal, in the famous third *relatio*, for toleration of a plurality of cults: because it is difficult to know about the divine realm, "it cannot be that there is only one way by which to gain access to such a great mystery."

31. *De cons. ev.* I.12.18, 14.21, 17.25, 19.27, 22.30, 24.37-26.40, 27.42, 29.45 ; *De civ. Dei* XIX.22-23, XX.24, XXII.3 and 25. All of these are seemingly based on Porphyry's commentary on the so-called *Chaldaean Oracles*, a second-century work which puts down the disciples as fools or magicians but has a better opinion of Jesus as a Hellenistic sage and gives high praise to "the God of the Hebrews" (Augustine summarizes many of its alleged oracles in *De civ. Dei* XIX.23). From *De cons. ev.* I.29.45 we learn that Augustine had also heard indirectly of the opinion of Numenius (known also through Eusebius' *Praeparatio evangelica*) that the God of the Hebrews is above the elements from which the corporeal world is made (cf. Numenius' famous statement, "What is Plato but Moses Atticizing?" quoted by Clement of Alexandria, *Strom.* I.150). For a comprehensive survey, see John G. Gager, *Moses in Greco-Roman Paganism* (Nashville 1972).

32. This line of argument would scarcely take the pagans by surprise; indeed, it simply confirms what they already knew about the exclusivism of the Hebraic-Christian tradition and rejected as a violation of the rules under which they operated. One of the most powerful statements can be found already in

Celsus, who attacks the Christians for misunderstanding the divine "enigmas," seeing warfare between God and a power opposed to him when the myths spoke only of the tensions between the various causes shaping the cosmos (*C. Cels.* VI.42), or for "dividing the kingdom of God and making two opposing forces" (ibid. VIII.11; cf. the passages quoted by Origen in the entire section, VII.68-VIII.67). Celsus is not surprised to find such views arising out of the tradition of the Jews, who rebelled against their native Egyptian heritage (III.5); in the same manner Gentile converts to Christianity have forsaken their own traditions for those of the Jews, as though these had a deeper wisdom (V.41). Origen, for his part, acknowledges the Christian belief that "those whom other men worship are not God's servants" (VIII.13) and that "we avoid those things which, though they have an appearance of piety, make impious those who have been led astray from the way of piety mediated through Jesus Christ" (VIII.20). There is a conflict of basic policy, impossible of resolution. Celsus and Origen agree, for example, that the daemons pose a problem, since they are interested only in earthly honors like blood, sacrifices, and magical spells, and their knowledge and power are limited to corporeal affairs; therefore they can distract one's attention from higher things (VIII.60). But Celsus goes on (VIII.63 and 66) to say that as long as the soul is directed toward God there is no harm in propitiating both the daemons and the earthly rulers who hold power through them, since the worship of God is more complete if one praises all these powers; Origen exorcises the daemons with the sign of the cross and refuses to swear by the fortune of any man, even the emperor.

33. Spatial diversity was especially a problem in Augustine's debate with the Donatists, who could claim with some credibility to represent the authentic "African" church tradition of Tertullian and Cyprian, while the Catholics were those who agreed with the overseas churches and their decisions in canon law (R. A. Markus, *Saeculum: History and Society in the Theology of St Augustine* [Cambridge 1970] 105-10). Augustine, in reply, taunted them for their narrowness and provincialism: "The clouds of heaven proclaim that the house of God is being built throughout the earth, and the frogs croak from the marsh, 'We alone are Chris-

54

tians'" (*Enarr. in Ps.* 95.11); "You sit and speak against not one brother but against all your brethren that are found among all the nations" (Ep. 93.6.20 to Vincentius, a Rogatist bishop).

34. On the two cities, see A. Lauras and Henri Rondet, 'Le thème des deux cités dans l'œuvre de saint Augustin,' *Études augustiniennes* (Théologie 28, Paris 1953) 99-160; Joseph Ratzinger, *Volk und Haus Gottes in Augustins Lehre von der Kirche* (Münchener theologische Studien, Munich 1954) 15-20, and 'Herkunft und Sinn der Civitas-Lehre Augustins. Begegnung und Auseinandersetzung mit Wilhelm Kamlah,' AM II, 965-79; Gerhart B. Ladner, *The Idea of Reform: Its Impact on Christian Thought and Action in the Age of the Fathers* (Cambridge, Mass. 1959) 256-66. The influence of Tyconius' *Book of Rules* and his lost commentary on the Apocalypse is discussed in Ladner, 259-66, and Ulrich Duchrow, *Christenheit und Weltverantwortung. Traditionsgeschichte und systematische Struktur der Zweireichenlehre* (Forschungen und Berichte der Evangelischen Studiengemeinschaft 25, Stuttgart 1970) 221-23, 232-34, 259-60. Alfred Adam has drawn together many parallels between the two cities theme (and even the *corpus permixtum*) and Manichaeism in 'Der manichäische Urprsung der Lehre von der zwei Reichen bei Augustin,' TLZ 77 (1952) 386-90 and 'Das Fortwirken des Manichäismus bei Augustin,' ZKG 69 (1958) 1-25, but the fact of congruences in imagery still does not prove the major influence that he supposes.

The existence of the city of God throughout human history is first asserted in *De catechizandis rudibus*, a model for catechetical instruction written about 400 (3.6, 19.33, 20.36). The motif is traced in Yves J.-M. Congar, 'Ecclesia ab Abel,' *Abhandlungen über Theologie und Kirche. Festschrift für Karl Adam* (Düsseldorf 1952) 79-108 and J. Beumer, 'Die Idee einer vorchristliche Kirche bei Augustinus,' *Münchener theologische Zeitschrift* 3 (1952) 161-75. Émilien Lamirande, *L'Église céleste selon saint Augustin* (Paris 1963) 69-73 suggests an influence from Nicetas of Remesiana, *De symbolo* V.10, which could have been mediated through Paulinus of Nola after 398. But Ambrose (Ep. 18.29) said even earlier that "from the origin of the world" faith and merit flourished among the saints, though they have spread among the peoples only in the last age.

35. Ep. 102, q. 2, nn. 10-13 and 15, and q. 3, nn. 18-19. For a general discussion of Augustine's views on the omnipresence of grace and the possibility of salvation in all times and places, see Joseph Mausbach, *Die Ethik des hl. Augustinus* (2nd ed. Freiburg 1929) II, 310-23. The groundwork for this theory of diversity is already laid in *Conf.* III.7.12-9.17, where Augustine defends the changes in moral standards in Biblical history by arguing that the law of justice always remains the same, but that God as sovereign can apply it in different ways, according to what is suited to the times and circumstances.

36. This is the point of the extended argument in *De civ. Dei* IX (esp. 15 and 23) and X. It is anticipated in all its essentials in Ep. 102, q. 3, n. 20, and it is already being assumed, without being fully verbalized in all details, in the passages on "false mediators" cited in note 28 above.

37. *De cons. ev.* I.37.47-32.50 (cf. I.16.24); *C. ep. Parm.* I.9.15, II.92.202-13.

38. The worldwide mission is already a theme in the New Testament (Mt. 28.20; Acts 1.8, I Tim. 3.16, etc.). Numerous passages from the patristic period are listed in Adolf Harnack, *The Mission and Expansion of Christianity in the First Three Centuries*, translated by James Moffatt (London 1908) II 1-32. In the fourth century the idea becomes a commonplace. For Augustine's earlier use of it as a sign of divine authorization, see note 23 above.

39. Cf. *De fide rerum quae non videntur* 4.7: "Look at these things, attend to these things, think about these things that you see; they are not past things that are narrated, nor future things that are foretold, but present things shown openly. Do they seem empty or trifling to you? Do you think this divine miracle to be nothing or a small matter, when the whole human race joins under the name of one who was crucified?" Markus, *Saeculum* 33 and 35, comments on the surprised—I would rather say triumphant—expression "ecce nunc fit" in *De cons. ev.* I.26.40. The "juristic" context of at least some of these passages is indicated by the earliest of them, Ep. 43.9.25 against the Donatists: "Let us not argue over ancient documents, public archives, or the

records of civil or ecclesiastical courts. We have a larger book, the entire world; in it I can read, already accomplished, what I read promised in the book of God . . ." What is now happening, because it was foretold, validates the contemporary claims of the Catholic Church against the Donatists and of Christianity against the pagans.

40. Passages arguing the fulfillment of prophecy in the spread of the Church include the following: *C. Faust.* XII.6 and 43; XIII.2 and 5-7; *De cat. rud.* 3.5, 6.10, 24.44-27.53; *De cons. ev.* I.16.24, 31.47-32.50; *De fid. rer.* 3.5, 4.6, 5.8; *C. litt. Petil.* I.13.14, II.32.73-74. In *De civ. Dei,* X.32, XII.11, XVI.9, XVIII.27-36, XIX.17, XX.30.

41. *C. Faust.* XIII.7; *De fid. rer.* 3.6, 7.10; *C. litt. Petil.* II.42.210-13, 132.210-11; *C. Cresc.* III.5.56; *In Joann. ev.* tr. 11.14. Two of the more complex interpretations deserve special note. In Psalm 2 it is first said that the nations rage and the kings of the earth rise up against the Lord and his anointed, and then they are commanded to be instructed and serve the Lord with fear (this appears in C. Faust. XIII.7, about 398-99, and it is still used in Ep. 185. 5.19-20 [*Liber de correctione Donatistarum*], about 417). In the book of Daniel, Nebuchadnezzar first prohibits the worship of the true God under penalty of death, but after his conversion he prohibits idolatry under the same penalty, thus becoming a type of the Christian ruler (this first appears somewhat later, in *C. litt. Petil.* II.92.211-12, written after 404, and the last use of it, I believe, is in Ep. 93.3.9 and *In Joann. ev.* tr. 11.14, both about 407-8).

The justification can also be purely rational. In *De cons. ev.* I.33.51 Augustine urges the pagans to read their own philosophers, whom they will find reproving the very things that are now being taken away, and thus implicitly praising Christian times, which are bringing behavior more into conformity with reason.

The general restraint of the Christians about destroying idols or despoiling temples, except when these have somehow become their property, is documented in Van der Meer, *Augustine the Bishop* 42-43. This, of course, reinforces Augustine's point that only the emperors have the right to stamp out idolatry and thus fulfill the prophecies.

42. Ep. 93.2.8 (written about 407-8).

43. *Enarr. in Ps.* 149.13 (preached about 411-13).

44. *C. litt. Petil.* II.92.211.

45. Ep. 232.3 and 6.

46. *C. Faust.* XXII.60; cf. ibid. XIII.7, where it is said that the kings of the earth subject themselves to "Christ the Emperor" (against Markus, *Saeculum* 37, who interprets *christianum imperium* to mean "Christian Empire").

47. An extensive literature on Church and State has grown up over the decades. See especially Erik Peterson, *Der Monotheismus als politisches Problem. Ein Beitrag zur Geschichte der politischen Theologie im Imperium Romanum* (Munich 1935, reprinted in *Theologische Traktate* [Munich 1951] 45-147; Charles Norris Cochrane, *Christianity and Classical Culture: A Study of Thought and Action from Augustus to Augustine* (New York 1944); Hendrik Berkhof, *Kirche und Kaiser. Eine Untersuchung der Entstehung der byzantinischen und der theokratischen Staatsauffassung im vierten Jahrhundert,* translated from Dutch into German by Gottfried W. Locher (Zollikon-Zürich 1947); Wilhelm Kamlah, *Christentum und Selbstbehauptung* (Frankfurt 1940), new edition under the title *Christentum und Geschichtlichkeit* (Stuttgart 1951); S. L. Greenslade, *Church and State from Constantine to Theodosius* (F. D. Maurice Lectures, London 1954); Karl Frederick Morrison, *Rome and the City of God: An Essay on the Constitutional Relationships of Empire and Church in the Fourth Century* (Transactions of the American Philosophical Society, New Series 54, part 1, 1964); Arnold Ehrhardt, *Politische Metaphysik von Solon bis Auugstin,* 2 vols. (Tübingen 1959); Per Beskow, *Rex Gloriae: The Kingship of Christ in the Early Church* (Stockholm 1962).

Although it may be rash to speak of "theories" of Church and State, the conflict of parties and the controversial literature it produced disclose three fundamental "attitudes" or "policies":

(1) A policy of religious toleration officially prevailed from Constantine through Julian and Valentinian, being revoked only under Theodosius. Pagan cults were allowed to continue, with some exceptions, and there was a trend to divest imperial offices of their old pagan functions without substituting Christian ones.

58

Although this policy offered the Church considerable freedom from governmental interference in matters of religion, it implied that the Empire could become religiously neutral and "secular," and this was not to the liking of most churchmen—or most of the emperors, either.

(2) Under Constantine and his sons there was also a tendency to create a mystique of the emperor as God's representative, not necessarily superior to the Church (though Constantius even attempted to dictate to councils), but at least on a par with it and effectively beyond criticism. The classic statement of this imperial ideology is in the writings of Eusebius of Caesarea, who has come under attack since the 1930's, especially by historians made aware of the implications of his position through their resistance to Naziism (Peterson, Berkhof, Ehrhardt).

(3) Especially among Christian leaders who happened to be on the losing side when the Empire involved itself in the doctrinal controversies of the fourth century—Athanasius, Lucifer of Cagliari, Hilary—there grew up a readiness to criticize emperors in strong language, and this heritage came to its climax in Ambrose, who successfully confronted emperors on several occasions and played a major role in shaping Theodosius' religious legislation.

Augustine's writings in the period 399-410 have appeared to some historians to be in the tradition of Eusebius (Duchrow, *Christenheit und Weltverantwortung* 292-93, sees pure "Reichstheologie" in *De cons. ev.* I) and Markus, *Saeculum* 30-42, depicts Augustine's thought as being dominated for a decade by amazement at the success of the "Theodosian establishment." Both of them recognize, however, that Augustine never contemplated a Christianizing of the entire social and political order, such that the heavenly city would be adequately reflected in the earthly realm. Markus points the way out of his own position when he says, "Neither in his dealings with imperial officials nor in his writings in defense of religious coercion did he ever consider Christian rulers and civil servants as parts of a governmental machinery, of the 'state.' He thought of them as members of the Church . . ." (148).

The elements of arbitrariness and intolerance that are undeniably present in Augustine's political ideal are adequately explained

59

by the Ambrosian type, without having recourse to the Eusebian. They are the result of an ineluctable progression of thought:

(1) In accordance with Romans 13, every soul is to be subject to the higher powers and render tribute to them (*Exp. prop. ep. ad Rom.* 72; *De cat. rud.* 21.37).

(2) This authority does not extend to faith and the worship of God, at least in the case of those who obey God's revealed commands. The exemption does not imply freedom of conscience for pagans, Jews, heretics, or schismatics (*Ep. ad Rom. inch. exp.* 15 and 19; cf. *De civ. Dei* XIX.17).

(3) A Christian ruler, instructed by the Church and obedient to God's commands even in those duties that belong to his office, escapes these restrictions altogether, for he must act as a son of the Church, and even in behalf of the Church, in suppressing error (see the passages cited in note 51 below). These actions also fall under the imperative of Romans 13 that "every soul" is to be subject to the ruling powers (note the use of Romans 13 in Ep. 87.7, Ep. 93.6.20, Ep. 153.6.19, and *C Gaudent.* I.19.20-21).

The fatal link is that *imperium*, under both the Republic and the Empire, was always acknowledged to include authority in matters of religion. Just as the pagan emperors had to respect custom, the Christian emperors generally respected the decisions of councils of the Church; but the power remained, and it was beyond question that *impietas* and *sacrilegium* were punishable by the public authorities (this is noted by Augustine in Ep. 185.5. 20). Although Christians could claim the right of conscientious objection against *pagan* or *heretical* emperors, on the grounds that divine law superseded human law, this principle could not be invoked against *Catholic* rulers, and thus the older Roman conception of jurisdiction continued on into Christian times.

48. Ernst Ludwig Grasmück, *Coercitio. Staat und Kirche im Donatistenstreit* (Bonner historische Forschungen 22, Bonn 1963) surveys from a legal standpoint the history of imperial concern with Donatism, from Constantine until the decisive events of 411. He argues that these measures were an extension of the power of *coercitio*, even when various legal prohibitions and penalties were added, and that contemporaries understood them in that sense. He shows that Augustine, like other Christian writers,

used technical legal terms when that was the context of argument, and that he clearly differentiated between "punishment" of the pagans and "coercion" of the Donatists (see esp. 189-90, n. 132; 193-94; 242 and n. 462; 246, n. 477). The distinction is explicitly made in Ep. 93.3.10; note also Ep. 133 to Marcellinus, where Augustine urges that, even though the matter is called "penal," it be executed in a "coercive" manner to turn them from their madness.

Augustine's autobiographical statement is found in Ep. 93.5.17 (cf. also 1.2), written in 407/8. I shall not go into the debate over the degree of change in his attitude toward the Donatists, or its exact chronology. The usual view is that he first rejected the use of compulsion as out of keeping with the freedom of belief, and even counseled against the use of force in self-defense against the violence of the Circumcelliones; then during the period 399-405 he agreed that this violence should be punished by the government, especially by levying fines on the clergy guilty of organizing it; and only after 405 he consented to the use of *coercitio* to lead the Donatists back into the unity of the Church (see Gustave Combès, *La doctrine politique de saint Augustin* [Paris 1927] 352-409; G. G. Willis, *Saint Augustine and the Donatist Controversy* [London 1950] 127-35; Herbert A. Deane, *The Political and Social Ideas of St. Augustine* [New York 1963], ch. 6; Peter R. L. Brown, 'St Augustine's Attitude to Religious Coercion,' JRS 54 [1964] 107-16).

49. Ep. 93.1.2; 2.4; 2.6-8; 5.16. The famous *cogite intrare* (Lk. 14.21-23) enters in this work (Ep. 93.2.5).

50. Ep. 104.3.8, in reply to Nectarius' Ep. 103. The argument is also extended to warfare, which can be waged out of love, with a "benign harshness" (Ep. 118.2.13) in order to restore peaceful association with those who have made themselves enemies. That this rationale for warfare, and perhaps for other measures using force or the threat of force, did not have to wait upon a change in Augustine's approach to the Donatist question is shown by *C. Faust.* XXII.74-75, written about 398-99, where Augustine comments that it is the entering upon hostilities that is reprehensible, and to respond is to preserve public peace.

61

51. Ep. 134.3-4 to "my son Apringius," written about 411. In Ep. 100 to Donatus, the proconsul, he urges that in all cases affecting the Church he forget that he has the power of capital punishment, since the aim is not the death of sinners but their deliverance from error.

52. Duchrow, *Christenheit und Weltverantwortung* 297; Albert de Veer, review of Grasmück's *Coercitio,* REA 12 (1966) 292-93; Hans-Joachim Diesner, 'Die "Ambivalenz" des Friedensgedankens und der Friedenspolitik bei Augustin,' *Kirche und Staat im spätrömischen Reich. Aufsätze zur Spätantike und zur Geschichte der Alten Kirche* (Berlin 1964) 46-52. Markus, *Saeculum* 204-10, makes an important distinction between parental rule, which would have prevailed even apart from sin and continues to be exemplified in ideal public figures, and coercion or repression as such, which belongs to those political institutions that arise because of sin. This may help to explain both the ease with which Augustine took a patriarchal view of government and the ambivalence which it usually exhibits in both theory and practice.

53. In Ep. 173.2-3, written about 414 or later, he acknowledges that the will is free and consent to grace must be freely given, but, he argues, the evil will is not free, and since it cannot be permitted to remain evil it must be liberated by driving sinners toward the good. Peter Brown, 'St Augustine's Attitude to Religious Coercion,' 111-12 remarks that as Augustine's doctrine of original sin and the bondage of the will developed, he became convinced that freedom of the will cannot be an unqualified norm for policy; the power of custom must be broken by a combination of external impingements and an inner evolution, all under the guidance of divine predestination.

54. Ep. 111.2 and 5 (to Victorianus, about 409).

55. *Retr.* 69 (II.43), and the letter to Firmus, edited by Lambot and first published in *Revue bénédictine* 51 (1939) 109-21; both reprinted in CC 47.i-iv.

56. Markus, *Saeculum* 37-38, cites passages from several sermons which indicate concern with *christiana tempora.* The point should not be over-dramatized, for Augustine had always reminded his readers that temporal prosperity or disaster cannot be a sure sign of God's attitude, and, on the other hand, triumphalist themes are

still present in *The City of God* (VIII.24, X.27 and 32, XVIII.50, XXII.5 and 25).

The City of God has been read and interpreted in a number of different ways—not only as an apologetic work, which is our concern here, but as a political theory or at least a Christian approach to politics, and as a theology of history or at least a theological perspective on history. Its high merit as an apology has been especially acknowledged by historians who come to it from a study of other apologists in the patristic period (see especially the classic work by J. Geffcken, *Zwei griechischen Apologeten* [Leipzig and Berlin 1907], who gives the Latin apologists generally higher marks than the Greeks and is superlative in his comments on Augustine (318-21); Cochrane, *Christianity and Classical Culture* 359-98; and Olof Gigon, *Die antike Kultur und das Christentum* 127-30). The apologetic nature of *The City of God* was asserted in former times, for example, in Heinrich Scholz, *Glaube und Unglaube in der Weltgeschichte. Ein Kommentar zu Augustins De Civitate Dei* (Leipzig 1912) iv and Ernst Troeltsch, *Augustin, die christliche Antike und das Mittelalter. Im Anschluss an die Schrift "De Civitate Dei"* (Historische Bibliothek 36, Munich 1915) 8-10, but almost incidentally, as if chiefly to prove that the purpose was neither to outline a political reconstruction nor to present a philosophy of history. The question has been examined more recently in J. Straub, 'Christliche Geschichtsapologetik in der Krisis des römischen Reiches,' *Historia* 1 (1950) 52-81; Eduard Stakemeier, *Civitas Dei. Die Geschichtstheologie des heiligen Augustinus als Apologie der Kirche* (Paderborn 1955); and John J. O'Meara, *Charter of Christendom: The Significance of the City of God* (St. Augustine Lecture 1961, New York 1961).

57. Serm. 105.6.8.

58. Ep. 138.3.16; Serm. 81.9; *Sermo de urbis excidio* 6; *De civ. Dei* I.23. Cf. *De civ. Dei* XXI.24, where Augustine says that the wicked city of Nineveh was destroyed in keeping with Jonah's prophecy, for the wicked city *did* fall, even though its walls and houses remained standing, and a good Nineveh was built up through repentance and conversion.

59. Serm. 81.9; *Serm. de urb. exc.* 6. Michael J. Wilks, 'Roman Empire and Christian State in the De civitate Dei,' *Augustinus*

I 505 n. 84, comments that this is an "ingenious reversal of the notion of eternal Rome." For Cicero's view that a city should be so constituted as to be eternal, and Augustine's reply that the city of God has a better kind of security, see *De civ. Dei* XXII.6.

60. Augustine himself mentions the first and more conventional theme, quoting a common saying, "The rains do not fall, the cause is the Christians" (*De civ. Dei* II.3). This is found all the way back to Tertullian, *Apol.* 40: "When the Tiber overflows its banks, or the Nile fails to flood . . . the cry goes up, 'The Christians to the lions!'" Cf. also Cyprian, *Ad Demetr.* 2; Arnobius, *C. Gentes* I.1-24; Lactantius, *Div. Inst.* V.4.3. But O'Meara calls special attention to the latter part: "The *City of God* is . . . directly more concerned with justifying the Christian prohibition of polytheism than with defending the charge of being responsible for the decline of Rome and its sack in 410 A.D." (*Charter of Christendom* 112), or again, "He could not be more explicit than he has been that the *City of God* is concerned with religion (XI.5), that his target is the cult of the false gods, and that the occasion of his argument is the prohibition of that cult in Christian times (I.14; II.2; VI.1; X.18, 32; XI.1; XIV.28; XIX.17; cf. *Retractations* II.43)" (104).

61. The general plan of *The City of God* is made clear in the text itself, and in the two later discussions of it cited in note 55 above. The first five books are an answer to those who think that the temporal happiness of the Empire depends on the worship of the traditional deities; the next five (VI-X) to the philosophers who assert that these deities are to be worshiped on account of a life beyond death. Then comes the discussion of the two cities, with four books on their origins (XI-XIV), four on their progress (*procursus*), or rather, Augustine says, their wandering course (*excursus*) through history (XV-XVIII), and four on their deserved ends (XIX-XXII). A detailed analysis is to be found in Jean-Claude Guy, *Unité et structure logique de la "Cité de Dieu" de saint Augustin* (Paris 1961). Roy J. Deferrari and Sister M. Jerome Keeler, 'St. Augustine's 'City of God': Its Plan and Development,' *American Journal of Philology* 1 (1929) 109-37 has some interesting though perhaps overly precise analyses of the way in which the plan is carried out and the degree to which Augustine digresses

to answer objections or investigate incidental questions (they calculate [126-27] that about one fifth of the pages are not immediately relevant to the argument). The number symbolism of the arrangement of books is explored in Joseph A. McCallin, 'The Christological Unity of Saint Augustine's De Civitate Dei,' REA 12 (1966) 85-109; he suggests that the two groups of five books symbolize the achievements of fleshly man (head and four limbs), first the political and then the intellectual, while the three groups of four groups each symbolize, respectively, the Trinity and the four corners of the earth which are called by the four gospels. G. H. Allard, 'Pour une nouvelle interprétation de la Civitas Dei,' Studia Patristica 9 (= Texte und Untersuchungen 94, Berlin 1966) 329-39 suggests that its basic arrangement—first the quest for beatitude, then narration of the history of the human race—is based on Augustine's catechetical practice, as seen much earlier in De catechizandis rudibus.

Burleigh has remarked on the apparent "air of unreality" that comes from the fact Augustine's polemic is based most often upon the classic Roman writers of the first century B.C.—Cicero and Varro, Sallust and Vergil. But this only lends to the work an added importance, as Burleigh then points out: "One has only to read the panegyrics of Claudian on Honorius and Stilicho to realize that he is in fact speaking to his own time. Classical Rome was still the Rome of the schools, of literature, of the vast company of rhetoricians" (John H. S. Burleigh, The City of God: A Study of St. Augustine's Philosophy [Croall Lectures 1944, London 1949] 44). He says elsewhere, "The apologist must meet his opponents on their chosen ground. His argument therefore mainly concerns ancient Rome in the days of her might and glory, security and prosperity, Vergil's City of destiny, the Rome of the grammarian, the rhetorician, and the world of letters . . ." (ibid., 168). The point of these remarks, of course, is that the debate concerns entire visions of the world, not isolated facts, and Burleigh suggests that "it is not altogether fanciful to see in the De Civitate Dei a countermanifesto to the Aeneid with its powerful and deceptive influence on the literary world" (ibid. 45). Indeed, the evidence shows that the Aeneid and other Latin classics began to be treated, precisely during the fourth century and in direct opposition to Christianity, as a kind of pagan Bible, and it is to this reverential attitude that we owe the survival of many of these works (see esp. the studies by Bloch, Cameron, and Syme cited in note 26 above).

62. F. E. Cranz, 'The Development of Augustine's Ideas on Society before the Donatist Controversy,' HTR 47 (1954) 215-16, notes that in the earlier period (up to 400 in his study) the two cities are understood purely in religious and moral categories, while earthly cities (including Rome and its empire) are treated as neutral. Markus, *Saeculum* 118, similarly comments that Rome was drawn into the scheme of the two cities relatively late: "Augustine had divided men into two classes according to their inner dispositions or their final destinies long before he faced the question: where does Rome belong in the scheme?" The use of the term "city" has aroused frequent discussion. Some of its resonances in classical thought are explored in Scholz, *Glaube und Unglaube* 71-81, though he is not very critical in evaluating actual influences upon Augustine. Ratzinger, 'Herkunft und Sinn der Civitas-Lehre Augustins,' AM II 969-73 stresses its background in the allegorization of Old Testament texts which mention Jerusalem. Ladner, *The Idea of Reform* 248, 267, 274-83, suggests that Augustine used "city" rather than "kingdom" because it was freer and broader, capable of including Church and Empire as well as the angels and daemons, and yet, in spite of this breadth, susceptible of differentiations between divine and human, good and evil, which a term like "kingdom," because of its connotations, would tend to veil in ambiguities.

63. Kamlah, *Christentum und Geschichtlichkeit* 168-69, notes the frequent opposition between "ours" and "yours": ". . . there is not a theoretical discussion, from a third point of view, about this religion and the other, but it is 'we' against 'you'" (169). André Mandouze, 'Saint Augustin et la religion romaine,' RA 1 (1958) 220, notes the passage in *Enarr. II in Ps.* 26.18 (about 411-12): "The father according to this world is the devil, and he was our father when we were unbelievers. . . . If he is the father of all the ungodly, who works in the sons of distrust, who is our mother? She is that city which is called Babylon; this city is the society of all those who are lost, from the East to the West, for she bears

66

earthly rule. It is after this city that a certain republic is named, the one which you now see growing old and diminishing; this republic was first our own mother, in her we were born. Now we know another father, God; we have forsaken the devil. How can he dare approach those whom the one who surpasses all things has taken as his own? And now we know another mother, the heavenly Jerusalem, the holy Church, one portion of which wanders as a stranger on earth . . ."

Alois Wachtel, *Beiträge zur Geschichtstheologie des Aurelius Augustinus* (Bonner historische Forschungen 17, Bonn 1960) 146, suggests that Augustine was making a direct comparison between the ancient city, always conceived as a cultic community, and the city of God, which is a society like the others but with different foundations (cf. Ratzinger, 'Herkunft und Sinn der Civitas-Lehre' 977-79).

Augustine's criticism of civil religion is especially striking, for he attempts to show that it is devised by men in the interests of the state. He makes much of the fact that when the books of Numa Pompilius giving the origins of Roman rituals were discovered, the Senate ordered them burned, as though the conscript fathers thought it was better for error to continue than to risk any disturbance of public order (*De civ. Dei* III.9, VII.34). He calls attention to Varro's veiled criticisms of this traditional religion —his confession, for example, that if he were founding a new city he would have based its religion on nature, but since he is writing about an old one he must follow its customs (IV.31, VI.4); and he hints that Varro, not daring to criticize Roman religion openly, set about to show its unworthy character by exhibiting it in all its unseemly details, under the guise of a pedantic antiquarianism (VI.8-9, VII.17 and 33). Yet Varro himself seems to have felt that it is "useful" for brave men to believe, even falsely (III.4, IV.27). It is not surprising that Augustine subscribes to the Euhemerist theory that many of the legends about the gods were confused stories about human benefactors (*De cons. ev.* I.23.32-33; *Serm.* 273.2 and 8; *De civ. Dei* II.5, VI.7, VII.18, VIII.5 and 26-27). He makes no mention of the imperial cult, perhaps because it arose after the classical sources were written and was no longer in existence in his time.

67

The contrast between the cities in matters of religion could not be more complete: the state exists prior to its civil religion, but true religion itself establishes the city of God (VI.4); Rome believed Romulus to be a god because of affection for its own founder, and this belief was fostered for the benefit of the state, but the Church has been founded by Christ through faith, and it loves him because it already believes him to be divine (XXII.6).

64. The refutation of classical politics and religion in the first part cannot presuppose, for its validity, the dogmatic presentation of the history of the two cities in the second part. On the contrary, the historical confrontation of the two cities can be understood only on the basis of a confrontation in the forum of reason between the eternal law, glimpsed more or less aeequately by the philosophers, and the lives of men. Guy, *Unité et structure* 77-78, suggests that the whole first part is intended to be preparatory, never proposing an act of belief but contenting itself with rational investigation or even, Guy suggests, a *récupération*—a recovery or retrieval—of the aims of sincere unbelievers, leading them by a kind of dialectic toward the city of God (30-31, 38, 40, 57, 70, 85-86).

65. In *De cons. ev.* I.33.51 (about 400), Augustine claims that the philosophers, by reproving superstition and the vice of the theaters, at least implicitly praise Christian times. In Ep. 91.3-4 (about 408) he says that Cicero gave a fine description of the ideal commonwealth and the virtues through which it flourishes, but he was not able to establish it (and again the bad examples portrayed in the theaters are singled out). The churches which are multiplying throughout the world, by contrast, are "sacred auditoriums for the peoples," inculcating sound morals and the worship of the true God. In Ep. 138, written in 411, directly in the shadow of the sack of Rome, and in answer to accusations that Christianity is inimical to the public interest and contrary to the mores of Rome, once again affirms the viability of the Christian precepts of love and says that the republic would have been on more solid footing if these precepts had been heeded from the start. They were never read in the temples or the public gatherings of the Romans; but they sound forth with divine authority in the churches, which function as "congregations of

the peoples, public schools for those of both sexes and of all ages and dignities" (2.10-11).

66. Ep. 137.5.17; Ep. 138.2.15.

67. *De civ. Dei* II.9, with Ep. 138.2.15 and 3.17.

68. The question of "political Augustinianism"—a tendency to absorb the rational into the revealed, the natural into the super-natural, and consequently the State into the Church—was raised by H.-X. Arquillière, *L'Augustinisme politique. Essai sur la formation des théories politiques du moyen âge* (Paris 1934, 2nd ed. 1955); see also his briefer 'Réflexions sur l'éssence de l'augus-tinisme politique,' AM II 991-1002. Arquillière, while acknow-ledging the *tendency* in Augustine, shows that the *political doctrine* emerged only gradually during the ensuing centuries. This aspect of Augustine's thought has usually been noticed by scholars whose chief concern is medieval political theory, for they, being aware of subsequent developments, are sensitive to their beginnings in Augustine, e.g., J. N. Figgis, *The Political Aspects of S. Augustine's "City of God"* (London 1921) 60-67; Charles Howard McIlwain, *The Growth of Political Thought in the West from the Greeks to the End of the Middle Ages* (New York 1932) 154-60; and most re-cently Michael J. Wilks, 'Roman Empire and Christian State in the De civitate Dei,' *Augustinus* I 489-510—perhaps the most intemperate of them all, carelessly reading back medieval ideas into Augustine, but at least doing the service of keeping alive the recognition that Augustine did see the divine law as laying a total claim upon life, with a "forced choice" between commit-ment and rebellion, and thus between the city of God and the city of the devil.

The issues are clarified most helpfully, it seems to me, by Berkhof (*Kirche und Kaiser* 189-90, 209-16) when he forthrightly champions what he calls "theocracy"—a view which he sees emerging in the fourth century and coming to a climax in Ambrose and Augustine —but differentiates it from a subordination of State to Church; theocracy properly understood, he says, means that the Church helps sinners on their pilgrimage toward the city of God and proclaims God's Word of both law and grace to all, including those who hold public office, even those who do not happen to be members of the Church, but does not attempt to bring everything

69

under her own control. Wilks, by failing to make the distinction, assumes that Augustine's underlying tendency is toward a "hierocratic" form of government (505).

In this connection it is useful to recall that Ernst Troeltsch, first in *The Social Teachings of the Christian Churches* (1911, English translation by Olive Wyon, London 1931) 201-7, and then in *Augustin, die christliche Antike und das Mittelalter* 26-51, drew a number of contrasts between patristic and medieval assumptions about the extent of the Church's influence upon society and showed that Augustine shared the basic assumptions of his age.

69. This is especially clear in Ep. 138.2.13-14 and 3.16. Cf. also the passages in which he says that temporal things must merely be "used" or "referred to the glory of God," who alone is to be "enjoyed" (*De doct. chr.* I, *De civ. Dei* V and XIX).

70. The full scope of Augustine's doctrine of law can only be seen from a work like Klaus Demmer, *Ius Caritatis. Zur christologischen Grundlegung der augustinischen Naturrechtslehre* (Analecta Gregoriana 118, Rome 1961), which traces the relationships between eternal law, natural order, and grace as the restoration of natural order (the work is made needlessly complex by an ongoing dialogue with Karl Barth over the sort of analogy that is involved in Augustine's manner of thinking). Cf. also Troeltsch's comments on what he considers Augustine's greatest achievement, the formulation of an "ethic of the highest good" (*Augustin, die christliche Antike und das Mittelalter* 41, n. 1; 49-51; 73-95; 105-12; 149-54; 173).

71. "Suum cuique (dis)tribuere" (*De civ. Dei* XIX.21; *De div. quaest.* q. 31). The source is Cicero, in numerous passages, perhaps especially those in which he defines all four virtues (*De fin.* V.67 and *De inv.* II.160-64).

72. The definition first appears in *C. Faust.* XXII.27 ("Lex vero aeterna est, ratio divina vel voluntas Dei, ordinem naturalem conservari iubens, perturbari vetans") and is repeated ibid. 30, 43, 61, 78. The same formula is used in *De civ. Dei* XIX.15 ("naturalem ordinem conservari iubet, perturbari vetat"). For a discussion of the definition see Cranz, 'Development' 300-301 and Markus, *Saeculum* 87-91.

73. See the discussion of "order" and "peace" in *De civ. Dei* XIX.13-14. Cf. also *De Trin.* X.5.7: The mind is commanded to know itself "in order that it reflect on itself and live according to its nature, that is, in order that it seek to *be ordered* according to its nature, namely . . . *under* him by whom it ought to be ruled, and *over* those things which it ought to rule." The proper order is always described as subordination to God, acknowledgment of the rights of others "in God," and subjection of the body and temporal things in obedience to God (already in *De doct. chr.* I.23.22 and 26.27).

Note the way in which Augustine, while acknowledging that man is both rational and animal, persistently stresses "rational" (*De civ. Dei* XIX.14 and 17)—not out of any delusion that man is an angelic being or can act out of cold calculation, for he acknowledges both the body (including the soul's love for it and desire for its resurrection) and the passions and affections (cf. esp. *De civ. Dei* IX.5 and XIV.6-9), but rather in order to counter the tendency to think of human nature as a kind of blind inevitability, highlighting instead the self-transcendence of the mind and the responsibility of the will.

74. In *De civ. Dei* II.19 he speaks of "that most holy and august senate (*curia*) of the angels, that celestial republic where God's will is the law"; in *Conf.* III.9.17 he even says, "That human society is just which serves you." Augustine often contrasts the "public" or communal spirit of the city of God with the "private" or selfish spirit of the alternative forms of society (*De ver. rel.* 46.88: "It is not surprising if someone who loves not the common good but a private good fails to attain the kingdom"; *Conf.* III.8.16: vice is setting the heart on one part of creation as "our own possession," whereas God ought to be regarded as "the good of all"; *De Gen. ad litt.* XI.15.20: "These two loves, one of which is holy, the other unclean, one social, the other private, one providing for the benefit of all on account of the celestial society, the other appropriating even the common good to its own power for the sake of arrogant dominion").

On the character of spiritual possession, see esp. *De lib. arb.* I.14.37, 19.52-53.

71

75. Cicero's definition, which makes its appearance in *De civ. Dei* II.21, is, "An assembled multitude associated by an acknowledgment of right and a community of interest." In that passage it is demolished, with a cryptic promise to return to the problem at a later point. This is finally done in XIX.24, where Augustine works out a substitute definition, "An assembled multitude of reasonable beings bound together by agreement as to the objects of their love"—a morally neutral definition capable of including the fully just society of the city of God as well as inferior societies, which may not be just at all. For a discussion of the varying interpretations of these passages see Jeremy DuQuesnay Adams, *The Populus of Augustine and Jerome: A Study in the Patristic Sense of Community* (New Haven 1971), Appendix A, "Augustine's Definitions of *Populus* and the Value of Civil Society" 123-35. (I am using Adams' term "civil society" as perhaps the best modern equivalent of *res publica*.)

76. This is emphasized by Demmer, *Ius Caritatis* 151, 190-92, 212, etc., who speaks of the city of God, the actualization of eternal law, as "event," and also by Wachtel, *Geschichtstheologie* 118, who suggests that Augustine's contribution to the theology of history is to show how the antinomy of eternity and time, ideal being and history, can be resolved by understanding historical structures as manifestations of creative being. (There is a similar resolution, though on rather different terms, in the notion of "idea" in Schelling and Hegel as not abstract and powerless but creative and filled with content, and therefore able to translate eternity into time.) When Wachtel suggests (51) that there is a "history" of the city of God only because of the fall of the angels —and of men—we should guard against an ambiguity in the term. The "history" of the two cities in the sense of an uncertain competition through time is indeed the result of sin, and Wachtel may be right in seeing Augustine's view of the six epochs of human history as a replay of the six days of creation, directed toward restoration of the original order (37-39). But even apart from sin the city of God would be "historical" in the sense that it depends upon the free enactments of both divine grace and creaturely response. In *De civ. Dei* XII.13-20 Augustine refutes the cyclical view of history on the grounds that both angels and men, as

72

voluntary agents, have indeterminate beginnings and act in time before they can be given a definitive beatitude. The importance of grace in the actualization of the eternal law can be seen in *De civ. Dei* XII. 9, where Augustine, who had wavered on the question for many years, comes to the conclusion that both angels and men were given the grace for a good use of their wills at the very moment of their creation, since it is unthinkable that they could have been created in a neutral state and then made themselves better than God had made them. The same is asserted of man in XIV.27; cf. also XX.17, where it is said that the city of God "has descended from heaven from the very beginning, in that its citizens have increased throughout the period of this world through the grace of God, coming from above . . ."

The role of free will in the origin of evil is, of course, a pervasive theme in Augustine's writings, from his early anti-Manichaean works to *The City of God* (especially books XII and XV). The dialectic of freedom in human history is especially complex. Just as the angels were drawn together in a holy fellowship to form one city of God by having God as their common good, the human race, which was to be united with them, was set in an intermediate position between angels and animals, so that they could either pass into the company of the angels without death, if they remained obedient, or, if they sinned, would become subject to death like the animals (XII.21). Adam is called the foundation of *both* societies (XII.27), the father of *both* lines, of Cain and of Seth (XV.17), because he contained in himself the possibility of both, and through his sin made all his progeny members of the earthbound city, from which many are reborn into the other city through redeeming grace.

77. *De civ. Dei* XIV.4, XV.1 and 8, "according to man" and "according to God"; XIV.1, "according to the flesh" and "according to the Spirit"; XIV.28, "love of self even to contempt of God" and "love of God even to contempt of self." Cf. also the passages contrasting the two cities in note 74 above.

78. *De civ. Dei* XV.1-5, and especially XV.2. This means that Israel, as a nation after the flesh, is a "portion of the ungodly city" (ibid. XVII.16)—though Augustine also calls her God's "republic" (*De cons. ev.* I.11.17 and 24.37). In *De civ. Dei* Au-

gustine discusses these complexities in terms of Paul's allegory of Sarah and Hagar; for clarification of the chapter, see F. E. Cranz, '*De Civitate Dei*, XV, 2, and Augustine's Idea of the Christian Society,' *Speculum* 25 (1950) 215-25, which has been acknowledged to be the authoritative interpretation.

79. The definition cited is from *De civ. Dei* XVI.17. It is true that Augustine uses expressions such as "the city of the devil" (XVII.20; XX.11) or "the daemon-worshiping city" (XVIII.41), but these are relatively rare. The earthly city, first and primarily, is made up of those who live in accordance with their own interests and desires. This in itself is serious enough, and Augustine in the first five books of *The City of God* concerns himself with the self-assertiveness of Rome, its attempt to build permanency and guarantee happiness on earth by responding to events in a constructive way, what Cochrane has called "creative politics" (*Christianity and Classical Culture* 83, 249; cf. Markus, *Saeculum* 83 and the whole of ch. 4). But in addition they are brought under the domination of the daemons through being deceived by visions and miracles, yielding to temptation, and being drawn together with them in a web of guilt, for "the devil cannot conquer or subdue anyone except through an association in sin" (*De civ. Dei* X.21-22).

There was a discussion some years ago among Charles Journet (*L'Église du Verbe Incarné* [Paris 1951] II 26-34), Étienne Gilson ('Église et Cité de Dieu chez saint Augustin,' *Archives* 20 [1953] 5-23), and H.-I. Marrou ('Civitas Dei, civitas terrena: num tertium quid?' *Studia Patristica* [= *Texte und Untersuchungen* 64, Berlin 1957] 342-50, over Journet's suggestion that there is, in addition to the two cities, a third, the city of man, with its cultural and political values. All agree that Augustine recognizes these values. But to him, as Marrou points out, "human" means "all too human," living according to man. Marrou admits that there is this area of human values in which the two cities are inextricably mixed, and he proposes the term "saeculum," on the basis of Augustine's occasional use of this term to denote the period during which the two cities interact within human history (*De Gen. ad litt.* XI.15.20). Guy, *Unité et structure* 121-22, prefers to use the expression "civitas terrena" in all its ambiguity as sinful human life called to citizenship before God; Markus, *Saeculum* 62-63, stays with Marrou's term because of the intermixture of the two cities.

80. See especially *De Spir. et litt.* 26.43-28.48 and *C. Jul. Pel.* IV.3.25—both contemporaneous with the writing of *The City of God*—where Augustine wrestles with this text. If it does not refer to the Gentile Christians, who do the works of the law through faith in Christ, then, he says, it must mean that even those who do not worship God properly are able to do some things which are commendable; these persons, however, do *not* have the genuine righteousness that comes by grace through faith, for their central motivation is not right and they fail to "refer" these good works to the glory of God.

Illumination by the Word continues to be viewed by Augustine as the basis of all awareness of logical and moral norms, even during the period in which he intensifies his understanding of sin in opposition to Pelagianism and, we might add, in opposition to the humanistic claims of the champions of classical culture. See esp. *De Trin.* XIV.15.21: "Where are they written, except in the book of that light which is called Truth, from which every just law is copied and transferred to the heart of the man who does justice, not through change of place but as by an imprinting..."

81. The wars of Rome are frequently called "just," or at least "more just" than the attacks of her neighbors which provoked them (*De civ. Dei* III.10, IV.15, XV.4, XXI.23), and this is probably said without irony, despite Augustine's suggestion that the Romans ought to worship as a goddess the injustice of other nations, since this is what enabled them to acquire an empire (IV.15) and his assertion that it would have been better to have a multitude of small nations living in concord (IV.15, V.17), for he genuinely believed that war could be waged with justice—even in love, by Christians—if it were for the sake of *restoring* concord with those who have made themselves enemies (see note 50 above, and the discussion in *De civ. Dei* XIX.12).

The virtues of the old Romans in the period before the Punic Wars are celebrated in book V, especially in ch. 18, where a succession of heroic acts is cited in order to deprive Christians—even the "holy martyrs"—of any grounds for boasting of their own sacrifices, since the Romans made even more dramatic ones.

Cf. Ep. 125.3 to Alypius (about 411), where Augustine uses the example of Regulus and other Romans to argue that Christians should not be excused for committing perjury under threat of death.

At the same time, it is made clear that these virtues consist more in heroic acts than in righteous dispositions, for they are not "referred" to God, and only this is the mark of "true virtue" (V.12). Therefore it would be more accurate to say that they "suppressed the desire for wealth and many other vices for the sake of this one vice, the love of glory" (V.13). Similarly in the case of the Stoics, who seek to satisfy only their own quest for integrity, their virtue, "if it is virtue at all," is merely for the sake of human praise (V.20). (Cf. Volkmar Hand, *Augustin und das klassisch römische Selbstverständnis. Eine Untersuchung über die Begriffe gloria, virtus, iustitia und res publica in De Civitate Dei* [Hamburger philologische Studien 13, Hamburg 1970] 24-27, 39-40, and the tabulation on 116-22, for Augustine's contrast between "true" virtue or justice and "their" virtue or justice.)

The crux of the discussion is Augustine's famous dictum (*De civ. Dei* IV.4), "Remota itaque iustitia, quid sunt regna nisi magna latrocinia? quia et latrocinia quid sunt nisi parva regna?" Its meaning depends upon the interpretation of the ablative absolute: Is it hypothetical ("*if* justice is removed"), or conditional ("*when* justice is removed"), or even causal ("*because* justice is removed")? Probably the second of these, for Augustine differentiates in the preceding chapter between good and evil rulers, and in the sixth chapter he says that to wage war through mere lust for domination can only be called a "grande latrocinium," in both cases leaving open the possibility for kingdoms that are *not* merely robber bands. (Cf. Scholz, *Glaube und Unglaube* 99-104, and, for a summary of more recent discussions, Hand, *Augustin und das klassisch römische Selbstverständnis* 61).

82. "They have their reward": *De civ. Dei* V.15. The Romans superior to their gods: II.9-14 and 29. Fulfillment of Roman virtues through correct worship of God: Ep. 138.3.17 (". . . that republic which the first Romans founded and enlarged by their virtues, when, even without the true piety toward the true God which could also have brought them, through a saving religion, to the

76

eternal city, they safeguarded none the less a certain integrity which could suffice for founding, enlarging, and preserving an earthly city. God has thus shown in the opulent and illustrious empire of the Romans how much can be accomplished by the civic virtues even without true religion, so that it might be understood that, when this is added, men are made citizens of another city, whose king is truth, whose law is love, and whose measure is eternity"); *De civ. Dei* II.29 ("This, rather, desire, O admirable Roman race, the progeny of Regulus, Scaevola, Scipio, Fabricius . . . Awake, it is day . . . Lay hold on the celestial homeland"). Wachtel, *Geschichtstheologie* 68-69 and n. 73, points out that Augustine correlates Abraham with Ninus, the founder, according to Gentile tradition, of the Assyrian-Babylonian Empire, and Christ with Rome; and just as prophetic passages about the gathering of the peoples are cited in connection with Abraham, their fulfillment in Christ is aided by Rome's bringing many peoples together as citizens of one earthly city (XVIII.22, 28, 45-46).

83. *C. Faust.* XXVI.3: "Man does not act against nature except when he sins, and even then he is brought back toward nature through punishment. For it belongs to the natural order of justice that sins either not be committed, or not be committed unpunished, and thus the natural order is preserved, if not by the soul, then certainly by God." *De civ. Dei* XI.17: ". . . as he is the most generous creator of good natures, so he is the most righteous orderer of evil wills." Ibid. XIII.15: "On the day that you eat from it, you will die" (Gen. 3.19) is interpreted to mean, "On the day that you desert me by disobedience, I will desert you by justice [death of the soul, whose consequence is death of the body] . . . Therefore it is agreed among Christians who truly hold the Catholic faith that the death of the body is inflicted not by the law of nature, through which God has never decreed death for man, but by the merits of sin . . ." Ibid. XIX.13 title: "Of universal peace, which is preserved by the law of nature through all disturbances, since each one comes, by the ordering of a just Judge, to what he has merited by his own will." Ibid. XIX.15: "By nature, in which God first created man, no one is the slave of man or of sin. But penal servitude is ordained by that law which commands the preservation of natural order and forbids its disturbance . . ."

77

84. For the most recent discussion of this question see Markus, *Saeculum* 72-104 and 197-210, and Duchrow, *Christenheit und Weltverantwortung* 273-88,. It might also be mentioned that in the classic essay by Ernst Lewalter, 'Eschatologie und Weltgeschichte in der Gedankenwelt Augustins,' ZKG 53 (1934) 33, there is a useful resolution of the debate over the "divine," "human," or "diabolic" origin of the state: "The *basis* of all coercive power is the sinfulness of humanity; the *origin* of this sinfulness is, however, the devil. The *source* of coercive power, by contrast, is providence, driving the human race toward earthly peace."

It seems to me that the often neglected key to Augustine's understanding of earthly law is *De lib. arb.* I.15.31-33, where he says that those who have an evil will cannot love the eternal law which condemns them and threatens penalties. But since they desire liberty and status and earthly goods, the temporal law allows them to have these on condition that they preserve peace and human association. As long as they are afraid of losing these things—and the threat is credible only because they love temporal goods, which can be taken away from them against their will—they will observe moderation in their use. The sin of loving these things is not punished by temporal law; what is punished is the infringement of the rights of others.

This perspective is the background of Augustine's theory of *coercitio* against the Donatists and of the doctrine of peace stated in book XIX of *The City of God.* Although certain changes have often been noted—Augustine states in this early work that temporal law must be derived rather evidently from eternal law (*De lib. arb.* I.6.15, 15.31), while he ignores that revolutionary notion in later writings—these changes should not be over-dramatized. In *De lib. arb.* I.5.11-13 he already points out that much of civil law is a concession to man's hardness of heart, allowing, for example, killing in self-defense, which is not permitted to the Christian in his private capacity.

Ernest Fortin, *Political Idealism and Christianity in the Thought of St. Augustine* (Saint Augustine Lecture 1971, Villanova 1972) 9 notes that Augustine viewed civil society as a structure that can "exploit man's perversity to its own advantage" by "pitting evil passion against evil passion." He also remarks (15, 48 n. 49) upon a certain similarity between this approach to civil law and that found in Kant's *Perpetual Peace* (we might now add the impressive work by John Rawls, *A Theory of Justice* [Cambridge, Mass., 1971], which acknowledges an indebtedness to Kant and others). But Fortin disapproves of the absence of morality in Kant's attempt to frame a political structure which could make evil wills live in civic peace and even justice. Be that as it may, the "political psychology" is the same. The chief difference is that these modern theories attempt to show how certain social and political arrangements can be based upon mutual consent among a number of self-interested individuals, all of them aware of the advantages they can gain—and the risks they run—by maintaining the rules of the game, while Augustine usually bypasses that whole discussion by thinking in terms of a wise, providential sovereign. Yet Augustine also recognized the existence of a social "pact" in which the members of the group arrive at implicit or explicit rules of distribution and retribution (see especially M. J. Wilks, 'St. Augustine and the General Will,' *Studia Patristica* 9 [= *Texte und Untersuchungen* 94, Berlin 1966] 487-522, and especially 499-515). Perhaps the chief qualifications that must be given to the "social contract" analogy are (1) that Augustine has a stronger sense for the social inclinations of human beings (*De civ. Dei* XII.21-22 and 27), and (2) that he sees them not as free agents in a contractual situation but as spiritual and physical dependents upon the shared values of the community, so that the important question is of which community one will be a member.

The problem of Augustine's attitude toward political life has often been discussed in terms of a distinction between the "primary" and "secondary" natural law, one for a state of sinlessness, the other for sinful man (Fortin 52, n. 98 cites the distinction in Occam and Hooker; it is made a tool of interpretation in Troeltsch's *Social Teachings* 153-54 and 195, n. 74, and also [though not by name] in a work upon which Troeltsch relied heavily, R. W. and A. J. Carlyle, *A History of Mediaeval Political Theory in the West* [3rd ed. Edinburgh and London 1930] I 144-46). The fathers, like Seneca and others, had to acknowledge that slavery, government, and private property could not be reconciled with the equality and fraternity prescribed by natural law except by seeing them as applications of that same law under changed conditions. Although they may be criticized for giving too much of an ideological justification for slavery, inequality, and repression, still they took their ideology seriously and did not merely acquiesce in political realism, piety toward human tradition, or subservience to the will of the sovereign. Therefore, I would argue, their theory remains intrinsically open to a criticism of all human laws and institutions, and thus to resistance, reform, or revolution, and it is largely a matter of judgment and decision—if not of prejudice and self-interest—whether one takes up the conservative or the progressive alternative.

85. *De civ. Dei* XIX.26. The text is first used about 398-400 (*C. Faust.* XII.36; *De cat. rud.* 21.37) as a sign that the saints are to be in subjection to the kings of the world and wander in exile until the end.

86. The question of the relation of the Church to the city of God has been dealt with in a vast literature, much of which is surveyed in Yves J.-M. Congar, ' "Civitas Dei" et "Ecclesia" chez saint Augustin. Histoire de la recherche: son état présent,' REA 3 (1957) 1-14.

In some passages Augustine identifies the city of God with the Church of the elect (e.g., XVI.2: "the Church which is the city of God"; XX.11: "the holy Church, that is, the whole city of Christ"; VIII.24: a house, the city of God, the holy Church, is being built in all the earth; X.6: "the redeemed city, that is, the congregation and society of the saints"; *Enarr. in Ps.* 98.4: "What is the city of God except the holy Church?"). In other passages he says that the city of God is in two "states," one heavenly and one earthly, and the Church is that "part" of the city of God which sojourns on earth and lives by faith (I. praef.; X.7; XIX.17). Perhaps the most careful formulation is found in those passages in which he identifies the city of God with the *heavenly* city, the city of God in its perfection, and then goes on to say that it begets and gathers together citizens on earth, in whom it sojourns in exile and yearns for its perfect state (e.g., XV.1: "the city of the saints is above, though here it begets citizens, in whom it sojourns until the time of its reign comes"; XIX.17: "the heavenly city, while

80

it wanders on earth, calls citizens from all the peoples, and gathers a society of sojourners in all cultures . . ."; XV.6: "the citizens of the city of God wander on this earth and sigh for the peace of their homeland above").

It is difficult to arrive at a formulation which can take all of these aspects into account. One admired formulation is that of Ernst Lewalter, 'Eschatologie und Weltgeschichte in der Gedankenwelt Augustins,' ZKG 53 (1934) 39: Augustine's point is "not to show that the city of God is 'the Church,' but to show the Church what she is, namely, the city of God in pilgrimage toward its completion." Étienne Gilson, at the end of his careful examination of the question in 'Église et Cité de Dieu chez saint Augustin,' Archives 20 (1953) 5-23, suggests that "the two notions of Church and city of God are not at every point identical" (21), chiefly because those who are not predestined belong to the Church in a sense in which they do not belong to the city of God, if the latter is understood as the company of the elect. But Émilien Lamirande, L'Église céleste selon saint Augustin (Paris 1963), demonstrates how often Augustine identifies the city of God with the heavenly Church and suggests that "ecclesia" is used as a proper term to designate the whole people of God, including men and angels, while "civitas" is a metaphor (9, 95-97).

It is generally agreed that even the earthly Church, in its most proper sense, is made up only of the elect, and also, because of the hazards of life in time, true believers who will at some time fall away. Those who are evil, and those who are not elect, only appear to belong to it. Augustine's earliest formulation is that the "Church without spot or wrinkle" (Eph. 5.27) has an inward and spiritual and secret communion with Christ (C. Faust. XXII. 38), while the others, who seem to be "within," are really "outside" (De bapt. VI.2.3; 3.5). In The City of God he says that these others are joined to the elect by communio sacramentorum alone (I.35), though even then, of course, they participate only corporeally and to their own damnation in sacraments which belong to the true Church (see especially Kamlah, Christentum und Geschichtlichkeit 145-47). Late in his career, as he resumes the early work On Christian Doctrine, he says (in opposition to the usage of Tyconius and to his own often vague use of the term)

81

that we should speak of the Church not as a "corpus permixtum" but as "the true and mixed, or the true and simulated, body of the Lord" (*De doct. chr.* III.32.45).

87. The entire context (XIX.14-20) must be taken into account in interpreting the discussion of slavery and government (chs. 14-16) and the episcopacy (ch. 19). The anticipatory enjoyment of the peace of the city of God in the "social life" of the earthly community is mentioned in chs. 17 and 20. For Augustine's understanding of episcopacy, and of ministry in general, see Michele Pellegrino, *The True Priest: The Priesthood as Preached and Practiced by St. Augustine*, translated by Arthur Gibson (Langley, Bucks. 1968). For the ultimate basis of this social conception, see the discussions of mediation and sacrifice, cited in notes 28 and 36 above.

88. *De civ. Dei* XIX.4, 20, 27; XXI.15-16; XXII.23.

89. Ibid. XX.7-9, 13. See especially Bernhard Lohse, 'Zur Eschatologie des älteren Augustin (*De civ. Dei* 20, 9),' VC 21 (1967) 221-40; also Émilien Lamirande, 'Le règne de l'Église et des saints avec le Christ, d'après saint Augustin,' *Études sur l'ecclésiologie de saint Augustin* (Ottawa 1969) 183-95, and, briefly, Duchrow, *Christenheit und Weltverantwortung* 260-64. This "reigning with Christ" is essentially reduced to being ruled by Christ, being his kingdom, and thus being associated with him; its chief benefit is the binding of Satan, who is held back from exerting his full power, but only upon those who are protected by the cross—and even this is taken away for the 3½ years when Satan is unleashed. Obviously the *regnum militiae* is quite different from the *regnum pacatissimum* of eternal life, and it is difficult to see how Augustine's position ever came to be interpreted as a triumphalist view of the time of the Church.

90. *De civ. Dei* XXII, chs. 5, 6, 7.

91. Ibid., the beginning of ch. 8.

92. The classic study is still P. de Vooght, 'La théologie du miracle selon saint Augustin,' *Recherches de théologie ancienne et médiévale*, 11 (1939) 197-222. As he shows from numerous texts—the latest of them drawn from book XXI of *The City of God*—Augustine thought that daily occurrences are full of miracles, both in the sense that nature has many inexplicable things which

82

cease to surprise us only because they are so commonly encountered (*De civ. Dei* XXI.4-5) and in the more profound sense that the great miracle is creation itself, with its many-dimensional dependence upon God (ibid. XXI.7-8). The miracles of Biblical history are treated as instances of this general miracle, and their uniqueness appears to lie chiefly in their function, that of arousing a vivid awareness of God, drawing worship back toward him, and symbolizing his salvation; indeed, a moral and religious criterion of this sort was indispensable to him, for he acknowledged that the daemons also performed miracles, for the purpose of attracting loyalty to themselves.

Many of the miracles of the martyrs are recounted in *De civ. Dei* XXII.8; a *libellus* also survives as Sermon 321 in the Benedictine edition. The epoch-making study is Hippolyte Delehaye, *Les origines du culte des martyrs* (Subsidia hagiographica 20, 2nd ed. Brussels 1933) 80-82, 117-18, 122-31. An important analysis of Augustine's shifting attitude toward Ambrose's miraculous discovery of Gervasius and Protasius in Milan in the year of his conversion, and toward miracles generally, is to be found in Courcelle, *Recherches sur les Confessions de saint Augustin* 139-51. See also Van der Meer, *Augustine the Bishop* 527-57, and Peter Brown, *Augustine of Hippo, A Biography* (Berkeley 1967) 413-18.

93. The discussion of the miracles of the martyrs in chapters 8 and 9 is enclosed in the broader context of a discussion of their faith in chapter 6 (which comes before any mention of miracle) and chapter 10. Cf. ch. 6, ad fin.: "The safety of the city of God is such that it can be retained, or rather acquired, only with faith and through faith; when faith is lost, no one is able to attain it. It was this thought, in steadfast and patient hearts, that made so many martyrs . . ." and ch. 10, ad fin.: "Let us therefore believe those who both speak the truth and work wonders, for by speaking truth they suffered, and so they were able to work wonders."

THE SAINT AUGUSTINE LECTURES

1959   *Saint Augustine on Personality*, by Paul Henry, S.J., Institut Catholique, Paris; New York, The Macmillan Company, 1960.

1960   *Platonism and Augustinianism*, by Raymond Klibansky, McGill University; unpublished.

1961   *Charter of Christendom: the Significance of the* City of God, by John O'Meara, University College, Dublin: New York, The Macmillan Company, 1961.

1962   *At the Origins of the Thomistic Notion of Man*, by Anton Pegis, Pontifical Institute of Mediaeval Studies, Toronto; New York, The Macmillan Company, 1963.

1963   *Augustine's View of Reality*, by Vernon J. Bourke, St. Louis University; Villanova, Villanova Press, 1964.

1964   *Augustine and the Greek Philosophers*, by John F. Callahan, Georgetown University; Villanova, Villanova University Press, 1967.

1965   *The Resurrection and Saint Augustine's Theology of Human Values*, by Henri I. Marrou, University of Paris; Villanova University Press, 1966.

1966   *St. Augustine and Christian Platonism*, by A. Hilary Armstrong, University of Liverpool; Villanova, Villanova University Press, 1967.

1967   *Saint Augustine on Creation*, by Paul Henry, S.J.,
        Institut Catholique, Paris, University of Califor-
        nia, San Diego; in preparation.

1968   *Augustine on Immortality*, by John A. Mourant,
        The Pennsylvania State University, University
        Park, Pa.; Villanova, Villanova University Press,
        1969.

1969   *Augustinian Personalism*, by Mary T. Clark,
        R.S.C.J., Manhattanville College, Post-Doctoral
        Fellow, Yale University; Villanova, Villanova
        University Press, 1970.

1970   *Augustine and Modern Research on Pelagianism*,
        by Gerald Bonner, Durham University, England;
        Villanova, Villanova University Press, 1972.

1971   *Political Idealism and Christianity in the Thought of
        St. Augustine*, by Ernest L. Fortin, Boston Col-
        lege; Villanova, Villanova University Press, 1972.

1972   *Augustine on Dialectics*, by Jean Pépin, École
        Pratique des Hautes Études, Paris; Villanova,
        Villanova University Press; in preparation.

1973   *Augustine's Strategy as an Apologist*, by Eugene
        TeSelle, Vanderbilt University, Nashville, Ten-
        nessee; Villanova, Villanova University Press,
        1974.

Publications of:

AUGUSTINIAN INSTITUTE
Villanova University
Villanova, Pa. 19085